QUALIFIED

SERVING GOD WITH INTEGRITY
&
FINISHING YOUR COURSE WITH HONOR

Dedication

To my daughter, Laura, and my son, Andrew. The joy you have brought me is unspeakable. I dedicate this book to you, and to all those in your generation who will lead by example and serve with integrity.

ENDORSEMENTS

Qualified is an excellent road map to a life of integrity and sustainable gains both for the reader and the kingdom of God. *Qualified* isn't a one-time read, but a tool for a yearly examination. As I enter my 50's my wife reminds me about a yearly check up with my doctor. A yearly check up isn't sought as a result of a current illness, but rather to prevent a catastrophic one in the future. *Qualified* helps us to examine the hidden parts of our lives, that if left unchecked can quickly become lethal in our lives.

John Nuzzo, Senior Pastor
Victory Family Church
Cranberry Township, PA

I have known and worked with Tony Cooke, both professionally and personally, for over twenty five years. He is a man of integrity, character and ethics just as he has written about in this book. How wonderful to reduce your life example to a written document. This excellent book about these characteristics should be mandatory for those in ministry, especially in the World today, when unfortunately some few lacking such qualities have focused negative national attention on ministries presenting the Gospel of Jesus Christ. I readily endorse this book and heartily recommend all readers, not just those in full-time ministry, adopt the teachings and practices portrayed.

Jim Guinn, CPA
Guinn, Smith, and Company
Irving, TX

We can't think of a more qualified person to write a book on spiritual leadership than Tony Cooke. We have known Tony for over 25 years, from the days as one of our Bible school instructors, to the head of our ministerial association and now as a minister pouring his life experiences into church leaders across the country and around the world. When Tony Cooke speaks on integrity, character and ministerial ethics church leaders would be wise to listen. We would recommend this powerful resource to every church leader as well as their staffs.

Jeff & Beth Jones, Senior Pastors

Valley Family Church

Kalamazoo, MI

Qualified is a must read for all church leaders and their staff. This book will provide a wealth of insight on what it takes to be a successful leader in the 21st Century. Honor and integrity are issues of the heart, and this easy to read book will inspire and challenge you to make these virtues the bedrock of your character.

Scott Robles, Senior Pastor

Victory Christian Fellowship

Fremont, OH

As a Pastor, I am constantly looking for valuable material to grow personally and to develop leaders. *Qualified* is an exceptional book that will challenge people to grow, empower them for service, and inoculate them against the common pitfalls of those engaged in Kingdom expansion. It is an invaluable tool for team training and personal empowerment.

Jim Herring, Senior Pastor

Abundant Life Family Church

Watauga, Texas

We as ministers search for new thoughts and insights, that we may in turn communicate life to our congregations. This book is a reservoir for the building up and sharpening of the leader himself. Tony has addressed a principle all leading servants must continually revisit: iron must be sharpened. It is imperative the Spirit of wisdom, discernment and integrity be developed in the leader's life. I crave life-giving tools like this book to refine in me the edge needed to stay effective for the Master's use. I am thankful for Tony Cooke and the way God has utilized him to keep the ministers of God sharp.

Rick Sharkey, Senior Pastor

Spokane Christian Center

Spokane, WA

Tony Cooke's book *Qualified* is a great book for anyone who has thought and wondered about the calling upon their life. It will help you to identify your calling, as well as strengthen it. Tony is an anointed teacher of the Word and you will be able to understand how to carry out your calling with integrity in your life. I believe that we all face hopelessness in our lives at one time or another. You will find comfort when you read this book, as it teaches you how to live out the call on your life. We all have a call on our lives and when we come to that realization, we can learn to live at peace with ourselves and with God. It is with great honor that I recommend this book to you. You will sense the presence of God as it is filled with the Word and the anointing. It will bless you.

Charlie Daniels, President & CEO

Daniels & Daniels Construction / Churches by Daniels Construction

www.churchesbydaniels.com

Broken Arrow, OK

Paul sent a message to Archippus in his letter to the Colossians: "Take heed to the ministry that you have received in the Lord, that you may fulfill it." This book will help you to do that. It is for anyone who is serious about fulfilling the manifold call of God upon his life. Like the scriptures, this timely message from Rev. Tony Cooke is also "profitable for teaching, for reproof, for correction, and for training in righteousness, that the man of God may be complete, equipped for every good work."

Joe Purcell, Director

Rhema Singapore

Singapore

Tony has given us a thorough and biblical reminder of the unique and serious qualifications required for God's ministers. In a season in which ministers are often valued for their charisma, appearance and talents, *Qualified* is a refreshing look into the heart and habits needed for the servants of God to finish their assignments with integrity. The prize is still awarded at the finish line and the principles which Tony reveals in *Qualified*, if embraced, will enable us to recognize and overcome the traps, temptations and tests which continually come to thwart our finish.

Eddie Turner, Senior Pastor

Family Worship Center

Murfreesboro, TN

The practical advice Tony gives in this book will be a great blessing to many leaders as they raise up the next generation of leaders. The scriptural foundation that Tony teaches will build strong and lasting leaders.

Sam Smucker, Senior Pastor

The Worship Center

Lancaster, PA

Every believer and minister of the gospel of Christ would be well served to read this masterpiece, *Qualified*. Within its pages, Tony Cooke has uncovered a wealth of biblical wisdom that will guide believers and ministers alike to run their race and finish their course with integrity and character.

Mark Thomas, Senior Pastor
Heart of the Bay Christian Center
Hayward, CA

It is my privilege to recommend Tony Cooke's new book, *Qualified*. This work is a treasure trove of insight and wisdom that has been first lived out by its author. This must-read book will enable and equip you to live a solid life and leave a lasting legacy. Thank you Tony for challenging us to live on a higher level.

Jonathan Del Turco, Senior Pastor
International Family Church
North Reading, MA

Qualified is a book that few ministers could write and go to bed at night with a clear conscience. I believe when it comes to reading on a particular subject you have to consider the messenger as much as the message. Tony gives this message substance based on his personal life and the example he lives as a man. As someone said, "The minister is only as good as the man!" *Qualified* is a must read for every "man or woman" to help preserve their character, keep their ministry safe, and maintain the right balance in life.

Paul Foslien, Senior Pastor
Living Word Family Church
Naples, FL

Qualified is a must read. Tony brilliantly lays out principles that every new Christian with a heart to minister needs to learn and the experienced person who wants to finish well needs to be refreshed in. He doesn't side step the real issues but hits them head on with scriptural examples and a heart for people. You will be encouraged, built up and strengthened as each chapter drives you to be the minister that God desires.

Dan Roth, Executive Pastor

The Rock Church

San Bernardino, CA

Qualified is packed with straight-forward and practical teaching that will equip and enlighten all Christians. Tony Cooke has done a fantastic job of searching the Word of God and showing us its application to our growth and success as leaders.

Douglas W. Holte, M.D.

Broken Arrow Family Practice Center

Broken Arrow, OK

TABLE OF CONTENTS

"...whoever in this way devotedly serves Christ, God

takes pleasure in him, and men highly commend him."
- Romans 14:18 (Weymouth)

INTRODUCTION

Years ago, one of the students in the Bible school where I taught came to me and excitedly told me about an opportunity that he had to work in a church after graduation. As he elaborated on the opportunity, I appreciated his zeal and enthusiasm, and in an attempt to affirm him I intended to say, "That sounds like a real gold mine." I was not thinking of money or wealth, but simply that this had the potential to be a great opportunity to learn and serve.

Instead, what came out of my mouth was, "That sounds like a real land mine." He was surprised at my statement, and I quickly corrected myself. Upon later reflection, I realized that every opportunity we have in life really does have the potential to be a "gold mine" or a "land mine," and our attitudes and how we carry ourselves often have much to do with whether our experiences are positive or negative.

This book is intended to challenge current and developing spiritual leaders. I have spent more than thirty years training Bible school students and working extensively with ministers across this nation and around the world. I have preached in more than 45 states and more than 25 foreign nations.

I have watched spiritual leaders rise and fall. I have witnessed some overcome the most incredible challenges while others have self-destructed. I have seen some fall away, while others persevered. I have also observed that some stayed true and on-track, while others were diverted on unproductive tangents.

My desire is for young leaders to avoid some of the pitfalls that have taken some of God's servants out of commission, and to see their progress accelerated as they walk in the path of the just.

We live in a day of skepticism and mistrust. Investment scams, widespread fraud, identity theft, corrupt business leaders, duplicitous politicians, gross media bias, athletic programs that cheat to get an edge, and abuse scandals in the church have seemingly become such a regular part of modern culture, that these types of incidents hardly surprise us anymore.

As greatly as I value the ministry of God's Word, the world will not be won simply by good sermons. Jaded, cynical, and mistrusting people desperately need to see believers who personify integrity, demonstrate godly character, and embody God's love.

If we are going to have godly influence in our churches, homes, neighborhoods, and in the marketplace, the challenge is the same - Our lives need to reflect the virtues of our message. The greatest challenge of spiritual leadership is not simply in knowing the right words to say or the right things to do; it is in becoming the right person.

All of society expects people carrying out important responsibilities to be qualified. Would you want to go to a doctor who was not qualified? Would you want to fly in an airplane where the pilot was not qualified? Would you want a mechanic working on your car who was not qualified? In all of these cases, such practitioners not only meet initial qualifications, but they engage in ongoing, continuing training to stay current in their respective fields. If those individuals strive for proficiency in their areas of expertise, how much more should those who deal with the souls and the eternal destinies of men endeavor to be as qualified and as effective as possible?

We will not be addressing all the technical skills necessary for spiritual leaders to be qualified, but we will focus on issues of integrity, character, and credibility that are necessary for God to be glorified and for people to be positively influenced through our lives and service. I want this to be the kind of book that pastors and mentors can use to sit down with those whom they are leading, and say, "Let's study this book together - it speaks to the issue of who God wants us to become as people."

I am writing *Qualified* because I want to see you succeed. I want people to see God's goodness and virtues in your life and in your service. I want you to serve God with integrity and finish your course with honor.

THE

QUALIFIED

LIFE

Chapter One

GOD CALLS - WE RESPOND

"You didn't choose me. I chose you. I appointed you to go and produce lasting fruit..."

John 15:16 (NLT)

Key Thought: *God calls us based on His plan and His purpose, not based on our perfection or lack thereof. His call is not an end in itself, but should launch us into a life of responding positively to His will for us.*

Julie Andrews, in *The Sound of Music*, made the following phrase famous, *"Let's start at the very beginning, a very good place to start..."*

Any thoughts about the calling of God or serving God, should begin with the understanding that our calling was initiated by God, not ourselves. He is the One who calls, equips, anoints, and appoints. It has been rightly said that "God does not call the qualified; He qualifies the called."

So let's start at the beginning and address the fact that God is the "initiator" of any calling that we may have in life. If God, who is the source of our calling, is one side of the coin - and rightfully, the first side we should consider - then we will not neglect the other side of the coin. The complementary truth is that we have a part to play; we were not created as mindless "marionette puppets," that automatically comply every time God pulls a string. He calls us and desires to work in our lives to qualify us for godly service, but we still need to do our part and participate in an on-going process of growth and obedience.

- We can respond or not respond.

- We can obey or not obey.

- We can cooperate or not cooperate.

- We can follow completely, partially, or not at all.

There is a sense in which God qualifies us by His mercy and grace; there is also another sense in which we become qualified, as we are faithful and diligent to follow Him and His plan for our lives. I've often pondered the words of the Lord Jesus when He said, "For many are called, but few are chosen" (Matthew 22:14). What is the difference between those who are "called" and those who go on to be "chosen"? Is it possible that those who are chosen are those who have cooperated more fully with their "Caller" and their "calling"?

If this book was only written about the "God-side" of the equation, then we would be ignoring our need to cooperate with God. Likewise, if we only focused on ourselves and our obedience, then we would be ignoring the One who is truly "the Author and the Finisher of our faith" (Hebrews 12:2).

We cannot recognize or fulfill our calling without God's help; however, He wants some level of cooperation from us in order for Him to bless our destiny. God doesn't demand flawless perfection on our part (none of us could ever be used if He did), instead He desires that we say together with Paul, "...we are fellow workmen (joint promoters, laborers together) with and for God" (1 Corinthians 3:9, AMP).

Processing the Call of God Upon Our Lives

In both the Old and New Testament, we see that accompanying any call of God, there is a process involved in order to bring that calling into full fruition. Let's take a look at an example of this process from David's life.

He also chose David His servant, and took him from the sheepfolds; From following the ewes that had young He brought him, to shepherd Jacob His people, and Israel His inheritance. So he shepherded them according to the integrity of his heart, and guided them by the skillfulness of his hands.

Psalm 78:70-72

People don't become stable, effective leaders overnight. There is a process involved, and we need to understand the essential elements of this process. In the above passage there are three key elements:

- **God chose David** - this speaks of God's sovereign call.

- **Integrity of heart** - this speaks of the development of David's character.

- **Skillfulness of hands** - this speaks of work done with competence.

Remember these three components: *call, character,* and *competence.*

Another way of remembering this is: *sovereignty, sanctification,* and *skillfulness.*

- God "sovereignly" calls us according to His will.

- There is a "sanctification" process that occurs, enabling us to serve with integrity.

- "Skillfulness" develops and enables us to do the job well.

All of these elements are essential in order for us to respond to and effectively fulfill, the call of God on our lives. Let's look specifically at the first element, which is reflected in the simple statement, "He also chose David."

The Sovereign Call

The Bible describes other sovereign "calls." For instance, God told Jeremiah, "Before I formed you in the womb I knew you; Before you were born I sanctified you; I ordained you a prophet to the nations" (Jeremiah 1:5).

Likewise, Paul said, "...it pleased God, who separated me from my mother's womb and called me through His grace, to reveal His Son in me, that I might preach Him among the Gentiles..." (Galatians 1:15-16). He also told Timothy that God "...has saved us and called us with a holy calling, not according to our works, but according to His own purpose and grace which was given to us in Christ Jesus before time began" (2 Timothy 1:9).

The idea of a sovereign call (relative to the initial call and the process that follows), is also seen in the way Jesus summoned His twelve disciples. Jesus did not choose the great scholars of that day, the great orators, or the great achievers. Instead He chose common, ordinary men, and through their union and fellowship with Him, they were transformed into world-changers.

> *And He went up on the mountain and called to Him those He Himself wanted. And they came to Him. Then He appointed twelve, that they might be with Him and that He might send them out to preach, and to have power to heal sicknesses and to cast out demons.*

> Mark 3:13-15

Notice the same three principles that we saw in Psalm 78 about David. A process springs from the initial call.

- **Call** - Jesus called those He wanted to Himself.

- **Character** - He appointed twelve, "that they might be with Him." It was their union and fellowship with Him that led to transformed lives and godly character.

- **Competence** - "...that He might send them out to preach and to have power..."

The call of God is not an "end-all-be-all" event. Rather, it is the launching pad to a working partnership with God from which transformation, growth, and obedience takes place in our lives. The issuing of a call is what God does, responding to that call is our responsibility.

Unfortunately, history is full of examples of God's call being unheeded. God said through Isaiah, "I have stretched out My hands all day long to a rebellious people, who walk in a way that is not good, according to their own thoughts..." (Isaiah 65:2).

Jesus expressed great sorrow and even wept over the city of Jerusalem, because they refused to respond favorably to the call of God that was expressed to them through His ministry. "How often I have wanted to gather your children together as a hen protects her chicks beneath her wings, but you wouldn't let me" (Luke 13:34, NLT. See also 19:41-44).

The communication between God and Isaiah is a good illustration of a divine calling that is followed by a favorable human response. In Isaiah 6:8 we read, "Also I heard the voice of the Lord, saying: 'Whom shall I send, and who will go for Us?' Then I said, 'Here am I! Send me.'"

People don't just randomly and arbitrarily step into great spiritual maturity or high ministerial offices. They are not automatically fruitful and effective, just because God called them. Obedience and faithfulness are necessary for those who are called in order for them to have a greater spiritual life and a productive ministry. There are many examples of people in ministry who received a call (e.g., King Saul, Judas, Demas, etc.), but ended up spiritually shipwrecked - not because there was something wrong with their calling, but because they did not properly respond to God in that calling.

God is a gentleman and He does not force people to respond to His call; however, whatever God calls you to do is better than what you have planned for your life. We may perceive God's calling on our lives as an event (although for some, it comes as more of a gradual awareness), however, we respond through a process of obedience and growth. This can clearly be seen in David's life.

When David was anointed to be the new king, it wasn't because he seemed to be the best candidate. If looks and appearance had been the key factors, then the nod would have gone to his oldest brother, Eliab. When the prophet Samuel followed the Lord's directions and went to anoint one of Jesse's sons as the new king of Israel, this is what happened:

> *Samuel took one look at Eliab and thought, "Surely this is the LORD's anointed!" But the LORD said to Samuel, "Don't judge by his appearance or height, for I have rejected him. The LORD doesn't see things the way you see them. People judge by outward appearance, but the LORD looks at the heart."*

1 Samuel 16:6-7 (NLT)

The Lord looks at the heart! What a profound statement. Men tend to look at charisma, education, social skills, talent, eloquence, etc.—and all of these can be helpful tools—but God looks at the heart! Centuries later, the Apostle Paul was reviewing some of Israel's history in a message, and he spoke of, "...David, a man about whom God said, 'I have found David son of Jesse, a man after my own heart. He will do everything I want him to do" (Acts 13:22, NLT).

In David's day, God was looking for a man after His own heart. I believe God has always sought such individuals, and continues to do so today.

The eyes of the LORD search the whole earth in order to strengthen those whose hearts are fully committed to him.

2 Chronicles 16:9 (NLT)

So I sought for a man among them who would make a wall, and stand in the gap before Me on behalf of the land, that I should not destroy it; but I found no one.

Ezekiel 22:30

You need to recognize, discover, and allow the calling and plan of God to be carried out in your life! It's okay if you are in the beginning stages of God's call on your life and don't know much yet. After all, God said, "Call to Me, and I will answer you, and show you great and mighty things, which you do not know" (Jeremiah 33:3). Enjoy your journey and all the discoveries that you are going to make along the way.

Questions for Reflection and Discussion

1. What does the phrase, "God does not call the qualified; He qualifies the called" mean to you?_____

_____

_____

_____

_____

2. What do Jesus' words, "Many are called but few are chosen" mean to you?_____

_____

_____

_____

_____

3. Do you believe that God called you to be His own and established a plan for your life before you were born? How do you think you have done in terms of discovering that plan? How do you think you've done in terms of the cultivation of integrity and skillfulness to facilitate expressing that call?

_____

_____

_____

_____

_____

4. The Bible says, "People judge by outward appearance, but the LORD looks at the heart." How mindful of this are you when you think about yourself?_____

_____

_____

_____

_____

5. What is the main insight that you have gained from this chapter?_____

_____

_____

_____

_____

_____

Chapter Two

CALLED TO
WHAT?

"There is a primary sense in which all Christians are 'called,' for Jesus Christ is Lord over all of life, over every task, over every endeavor. But there is another sense in which only some are 'called' to fulfill those special responsibilities and ministries set forth in Scripture on which the life and order of the church directly depend."[1]

- Sam Storms

Key Thought: *God calls us all to be His children, and gives us specific assignments as well.*

Since the time that God called out to wayward Adam, "Where are you?" (Genesis 3:9), God has been calling out to men and women throughout the ages, beckoning them to return to Him and calling them into His family.

Misconceptions abound concerning what it means to be "called" by God. Many Christians tend to think of the "calling" as something that applies only to preachers, but God has called all of us to be His children and to reflect His glory and honor in the earth. Has God called you to be:

---

[1]Storms, Sam, Are You Called to Ministry, Part 1, Enjoying God Ministries.com, November 8, 2006. http://www.enjoyinggodministries.com/article/are-you-called-to-ministry-part-i/

- A godly husband or wife?

- A person who will have a godly influence on his neighbors, friends, and co-workers in the marketplace?

- A productive worker or leader in the local church?

- A parent who raises children in the nurture and admonition of the Lord?

All of these are valuable and significant assignments in life, whether you ever step behind a pulpit or not.

We are supposed to serve God...

- with or without a title

- with or without a position

- visibly or behind the scenes

- through structure or spontaneously

- formally or informally

Some people think that a calling is always going to be highly dramatic and sensational. For some, it might be; however, for most believers, a calling can simply come as an awareness or a growing desire within their heart that turns them toward God.

Most believers have probably recognized God calling them to be His children - when they heard the gospel and sensed the Holy Spirit tugging at their hearts. We have heard of and rejoice in stories of very dramatic conversions, where individuals had a dramatic salvation experience (such as what Paul had in Acts 9:1-18). However, most believers don't usually have such sensational and dramatic experiences.

In my personal life, my call to the ministry was not dramatic or sensational. I did not hear an audible voice, have a vision, or see angels. For me, there was simply a growing awareness and an increasing desire to serve God that I had never experienced before.

Likewise, when it comes to being called to a specific function, most believers have probably sensed a desire to serve God in a certain capacity. As they were faithful, they started to notice that they had a certain aptitude or giftedness in their life. As they continued to be faithful, their aptitude or giftedness developed into greater proficiency.

Speaking of obedience to the will of God, Paul told one group of believers, "[Not in your own strength] for it is God Who is all the while effectually at work in you [energizing and creating in you the power and desire], both to will and to work for His good pleasure and satisfaction and delight" (Philippians 2:13, AMP).

Even when it comes to being a child of God, He has called us to some specific things; He hasn't just called us generically and in nondescript ways. As you consider the following verses, don't just skim over them, but look carefully to see exactly what God has called us to.

> *...you also are the called of Jesus Christ; To all who are in Rome, beloved of God, called to be saints.*
>
> Romans 1:6-7

> *...whom He predestined, these He also called; whom He called, these He also justified; and whom He justified, these He also glorified.*
>
> Romans 8:30

> *...called to be saints, with all who in every place call on the name of Jesus Christ our Lord, both theirs and ours...*
>
> 1 Corinthians 1:2

...you were called into the fellowship of His Son, Jesus Christ our Lord.

1 Corinthians 1:9

...Him who called you in the grace of Christ...

Galatians 1:6

For you, brethren, have been called to liberty...

Galatians 5:13

...but as He who called you is holy, you also be holy in all your conduct...

1 Peter 1:15

But you are a chosen generation, a royal priesthood, a holy nation, His own special people, that you may proclaim the praises of Him who called you out of darkness into His marvelous light...

1 Peter 2:9

...the God of all grace, who called us to His eternal glory by Christ Jesus...

1 Peter 5:10

To those who are called, sanctified by God the Father, and preserved in Jesus Christ...

Jude 1

Being called by God in no way speaks of our perfection, but rather, reflects His goodness and mercy toward us. While we were lost and separated from God, He chose to reach out to us because of how wonderful He is. When we think of the fact that God has called us to be His own, we should not be proud, but rather humbled and thankful.

Different Types of Callings

In studying the Scriptures, it becomes apparent that there are different types of callings. We just read numerous scriptures that apply to all of God's children. This type of general and inclusive calling is reflected in Jesus' statement (note, He says this is for anyone), "If anyone thirsts, let him come to Me and drink" (John 7:37).

There are also other types of callings that are unique to different individuals. These callings are not for everyone, but for those whom God has specifically called and chosen for specific tasks. For example, when Jesus chose His twelve disciples (who eventually became apostles), He didn't take volunteers. Mark 3:13 says that Jesus, "...called to Him those He Himself wanted."

We must respect the fact that God chooses certain people to do certain things. Hebrews 5:4-5 (NLT) says, "And no one can become a high priest simply because he wants such an honor. He must be called by God for this work, just as Aaron was. That is why Christ did not honor himself by assuming he could become High Priest. No, he was chosen by God..."

When it comes to being a child of God, He has called all of us - whosoever will - to partake of His grace and forgiveness. However, when it comes to ministerial assignments, the Scriptures indicate that God has different callings and assignments for each of us, and these are established at His discretion.

But now God has set the members, each one of them, in the body just as He pleased.

1 Corinthians 12:18

Now you are the body of Christ, and members individually. And God has appointed these in the church: first apostles, second prophets, third teachers, after that miracles, then gifts of healings, helps, administrations, varieties of tongues.

1 Corinthians 12:27-28

For as we have many members in one body, but all the members do not have the same function, so we, being many, are one body in Christ, and individually members of one another. Having then gifts differing according to the grace that is given to us, let us use them: if prophecy, let us prophesy in proportion to our faith; or ministry, let us use it in our ministering; he who teaches, in teaching; he who exhorts, in exhortation; he who gives, with liberality; he who leads, with diligence; he who shows mercy, with cheerfulness.

Romans 12:4-8

In regard to the ministry gifts of Christ - apostles, prophets, evangelists, pastors, and teachers - the Apostle Paul specifically states that, "He [Jesus] Himself gave..." these gifts to the Church (Ephesians 4:11).

Finally, the Apostle Peter also recognized a distinction in the functions of these gifts when he said:

As each one has received a gift, minister it to one another, as good stewards of the manifold grace of God. If anyone speaks, let him speak as the oracles of God. If anyone ministers, let him do it as with the ability which God supplies, that in all things God may be glorified through Jesus Christ, to whom belong the glory and the dominion forever and ever. Amen.

1 Peter 4:10-11

The Holy Spirit will not only bear witness with your heart that you are a child of God (Romans 8:16), but He will also give you the gifts and the spiritual equipment to do what He has called you to do. The Holy Spirit will also work through others to confirm and encourage you in your calling.

Now in the church that was at Antioch there were certain prophets and teachers: Barnabas, Simeon who was called Niger, Lucius of Cyrene, Manaen who had been brought up with Herod the tetrarch, and Saul. As they ministered to the Lord and fasted, the Holy Spirit said, "Now separate to Me Barnabas and Saul for the work to which I have called them." Then, having fasted and prayed, and laid hands on them, they sent them away.

Acts 13:1-3

Notice that these other men did not call Barnabas and Saul into the ministry; they had already been called by God. They simply acknowledged their calling and recognized that it was now time for Barnabas and Saul to begin doing what the Lord had already called them to do. Their calling was also confirmed by the fruit and the results that were produced as they obeyed God and carried out His assignment. Barnabas and Saul (later known as Paul) responded to God's call. They said, "yes" to God, and that is what we must also do.

Questions for Reflection and Discussion

1. In your life, did the call of God come to you more as an "event," or has it been recognized more subtly and gradually, as a "process" of being drawn to Him and having a growing awareness of a desire to do His will?

_____

_____

_____

_____

2. Go back over the list of scriptures at the beginning of this chapter (beginning with Romans 1:6 and ending with Jude 1), and ask yourself this question: How many ramifications of the calling of God identified in these scriptures have been and are being realized in my life?

_____

_____

_____

_____

3. Do you recognize the difference between callings that apply to all believers, as opposed to those that are unique to individuals, in terms of their specific assignments?_____

_____

_____

_____

4. What is the main insight that you have gained from this chapter?

_____

_____

_____

_____

Chapter Three

BUT I DON'T FEEL QUALIFIED!

"He who grows in grace remembers that he is but dust, and he therefore does not expect his fellow Christians to be anything more. He overlooks ten thousand of their faults, because he knows his God overlooks twenty thousand in his own case. He does not expect perfection in the creature, and, therefore, he is not disappointed when he does not find it... When our virtues become more mature, I trust we shall not be more tolerant of evil, but we shall be more tolerant of infirmity, more hopeful for the people of God, and certainly less arrogant in our criticisms. Sweetness towards sinners is another sign of ripeness."[2]

- Charles H. Spurgeon

Key Thought: *If God had to wait until we were perfect to use us, no one would ever be used by God.*

Have you ever struggled with the feeling of not being good enough to be used by God? You're not alone. Reflect on Paul's words to the Corinthians.

---

[2]Spurgeon, Charles, "Ripe Fruit" *The Metropolitan Tabernacle Pulpit, Volume 16* (1870), Sermon 945. Found at http://tollelege.wordpress.com/2011/11/20/he-who-grows-in-grace-by-charles-spurgeon/

Remember, dear brothers and sisters, that few of you were wise in the world's eyes or powerful or wealthy when God called you. Instead, God chose things the world considers foolish in order to shame those who think they are wise. And he chose things that are powerless to shame those who are powerful. God chose things despised by the world, things counted as nothing at all, and used them to bring to nothing what the world considers important. As a result, no one can ever boast in the presence of God.

1 Corinthians 1:26-29(NLT)

God has only called one perfect person, and that was the Lord Jesus Christ. Everyone else God has ever called to do something for Him - including you and me - has been a very fallible and flawed individual. God knows our exact condition when He calls us, and He starts with us - right where we are. The mercy and grace of God have caused many who did not seem to be great "candidates" for spiritual leadership, to undergo amazing transformations:

- Moses the Murderer became the Mighty Deliverer.

- Gideon the Insecure became the Lord's Warrior.

- David the Adulterer became the Sweet Psalmist of Israel.

- Peter the Denier became the Proclaimer of Pentecost.

- John the Boisterous became the Apostle of Love.

- Saul the Terrorist became the Apostle of Grace.

- Mark the Quitter became Profitable for the Ministry.

Biblical accounts reveal that those who God called to service often felt unqualified and incapable.

Consider Moses

When the Lord appeared to Moses and commissioned him to deliver the children of Israel from Egyptian bondage, Moses offered several excuses that revealed his shock and insecurity:

- He asked God, *"Who am I that I should go to Pharaoh...?"* (Exodus 3:11).

- He questioned, *"But suppose they will not believe me or listen to my voice..."* (Exodus 4:2).

- *"O Lord, I'm not very good with words. I never have been, and I'm not now, even though you have spoken to me. I get tongue-tied, and my words get tangled"* (Exodus 4:10, NLT).

No Bible-believing person would ever doubt that Moses had a call of God on his life, but some assume that Moses had no realization of his calling until the burning bush incident when he was eighty years old (Exodus 3). However, as a much younger man, Moses had an awareness of God's purpose for his life. He seemed to have grasped a general idea about his destined role, but he had not fully comprehended the vital details about the timing and the method of how his calling would be fulfilled.

Now when he was forty years old, it came into his heart to visit his brethren, the children of Israel. And seeing one of them suffer wrong, he defended and avenged him who was oppressed, and struck down the Egyptian. For he supposed that his brethren would have understood that God would deliver them by his hand, but they did not understand.

Acts 7:23-25

As you may recall the rest of the story, when Moses discovered that his crime of murder was known, he fled and spent the next forty years in the wilderness. Perhaps Moses' earlier dream of God using him to deliver the Israelites had died during four decades of hot days and cold nights in the Midian desert, but God resurrected those earlier perceptions, brought clarification to them, and gave him an amazing assignment.

Perhaps you are like Moses. You had an idea from God and you made an unsuccessful attempt to do something for Him, not realizing that you had the wrong timing or the wrong method. When you acted on that idea, things did not work well, so you threw in the towel. God wants us to serve Him, just like Moses did, but it's necessary that we do things His way and in His timing (this often includes a season of considerable preparation).

A huge key in beginning to cooperate with God involves getting our eyes off of ourselves. Why God chose Moses is God's business. We realize that God did not call Moses because he was perfect. Rather, God called Moses because of His love for the Israelites and His desire to liberate them. Before Moses could ever step into his destiny, he had to get his eyes off of himself and forget about his past. He had to focus on God, the assignment God had given him, and the people God wanted to deliver.

Moses finally understood that being called was based on the grace of the caller, and not the perfection of the one being called. He said to the people, "The LORD did not set His love on you nor choose you because you were more in number than any other people, for you were the least of all peoples..." (Deuteronomy 7:7).

Many Others Felt Unqualified

Gideon felt unqualified because of the inferiority that he felt due to his low socio-economic background. In Judges 6:15 he said, "O my Lord, how can I save Israel? Indeed my clan is the weakest in Manasseh, and I am the least in my father's house."

- Jeremiah felt like he was too young (Jeremiah 1:6).

- Sarah thought that she was too old (Genesis 18:12).

- When the Lord appeared to Isaiah, he said, "Woe is me, for I am undone! Because I am a man of unclean lips..." (Isaiah 6:5).

- When Peter encountered Jesus, Peter's response was, "Depart from me, for I am a sinful man, O Lord!" (Luke 5:8).

- Paul said of himself, "I'm not even worthy to be called an apostle after the way I persecuted God's church" (1 Corinthians 15:9, NLT).

Paul told Timothy that God, "...has saved us and called us with a holy calling, not according to our works, but according to His own purpose and grace which was given to us in Christ Jesus before time began" (2 Timothy 1:9). Paul knew that Timothy had certain fears and insecurities, and he wanted this young minister to understand, "Timothy, this isn't about you or how perfect or imperfect you are. Get your eyes off of yourself - quit dwelling on your flaws and your shortcomings - and get your eyes on the purpose and grace of God for your life."

Paul was keenly aware that his own background was not pristine. He said:

And I thank Christ Jesus our Lord who has enabled me, because He counted me faithful, putting me into the ministry, although I was formerly a blasphemer, a persecutor, and an insolent man; but I obtained mercy because I did it ignorantly in unbelief. And the grace of our Lord was exceedingly abundant, with faith and love which are in Christ Jesus.

1 Timothy 1:12-14

Has something held you back?

- Have you ever felt "unqualified" to be used by God?

- Are you considering yourself "unworthy," because of some deficiency in your skills or sin in your past, or even because of some struggle you are having in your life right now?

- Is there insecurity or a sense of inferiority that has kept you from yielding your life to God and His purpose for your life?

If so, as we said earlier, then you have a lot of company. We should never forget that we are privileged to serve God, and it is only by His mercy and grace that we can do so. Consider some important scriptures that reveal Paul's insights into the origin and nature of his ministry, and notice that his past did not keep him from stepping into his future.

For I am the least of the apostles, who am not worthy to be called an apostle, because I persecuted the church of God. But by the grace of God I am what I am, and His grace toward me was not in vain; but I labored more abundantly than they all, yet not I, but the grace of God which was with me.

1 Corinthians 15:9-10

It is not that we think we are qualified to do anything on our own. Our qualification comes from God. He has enabled us to be ministers of his new covenant...

2 Corinthians 3:5-6 (NLT)

Not that I have already attained, or am already perfected; but I press on, that I may lay hold of that for which Christ Jesus has also laid hold of me. Brethren, I do not count myself to have apprehended; but one thing I do, forgetting those things which are behind and reaching forward to those things which are ahead...

Philippians 3:12-13

What are some of the key ideas that governed Paul's perspective of his ministry?

1. Paul never forgot where he had come from. He recognized that God had not called him because he had been perfect, but in spite of his hostility against Jesus.

2. Grace was not only the basis for God saving Paul, but also the basis for Paul's enablement in ministry.

3. While grace was the basis for Paul's ministry, Paul himself worked hard. He recognized that his work was not independent of God, but in conjunction with God's work in him.

4. Paul recognized that God was the One who both qualified and enabled him to be a minister.

5. Paul did not consider himself perfect or as having arrived. He realized there was still more, and he was reaching for God's best.

The work that we do for God is not based on our perfection, but His mercy and grace. All of us are a "work in progress." It's not where we have been that matters; it's where we are headed now that counts. Your past is no excuse to keep you from the future that God has for you. God has a work for you to do, and what Jesus said in Luke 9:62 is true for us today: "Anyone who puts a hand to the plow and then looks back is not fit for the Kingdom of God."

Questions for Reflection and Discussion

1. Have you ever felt "unqualified" to serve God because of something in your past? What were your impressions as you read about individuals from the Bible that God used in spite of their flaws and imperfections?

_____

_____

_____

_____

_____

_____

_____

2. Have you ever done anything similar to Moses? Maybe you had the right idea about something that God was wanting you to do, but perhaps had the wrong timing or the wrong method? Were you able to recover from that and make the necessary adjustments to begin again more wisely?

_____

_____

_____

_____

_____

_____

_____

3. Describe, in your own words, how Paul saw himself in the light of his past failures AND the mercy and grace of God, which enabled him to become an effective worker and spiritual leader._____

_____

_____

_____

_____

_____

_____

_____

4. What is the main insight that you have gained from this chapter?

_____

_____

_____

_____

_____

_____

_____

Chapter Four

CHARACTERISTICS OF THE QUALIFIED

"Our Lord made clear to James and John that high position in the Kingdom of God is reserved for those whose hearts - even the secret places where no one else probes - are qualified."[3]

- Oswald Sanders

Key Thought: *All spiritual leaders should apply themselves diligently to becoming and staying qualified.*

I f we call ourselves into service - if we are "self-appointed" - then we would have the right to determine our own standards. But if God calls us into service, then we are accountable to Him and He has the right to establish what qualifies us to serve Him effectively.

Moses was at a point of complete overload. He was trying to single-handedly be the executive, legislative, and judicial branches of Israel's government. His father-in-law, Jethro, gave insightful counsel concerning the helpers he was to choose (Exodus 18:21):"...you shall select from all the people able men, such as fear God, men of truth, hating covetousness..." The Message version renders these qualifying traits as, "competent men—men who fear God, men of integrity, men who are incorruptible."

---

[3] Sanders, J. Oswald, *Spiritual Leadership*, Second Revision (Chicago: Moody Press, 1994), 19.

Was just anyone qualified to serve as a judge under Moses' leadership? No, the following common sense qualities were identified:

- They had to be capable and competent.

- They had to be God-fearing.

- They had to be people of honesty and integrity.

- They had to be incorruptible, hating covetousness and immune to bribery.

Those who were selected to serve in highly responsible positions had to embody credibility and integrity, lest corruption and injustice overtake God's covenant people. Many years later, King David said, "He who rules over men must be just, ruling in the fear of God" (2 Samuel 23:3).

In Acts 6, the apostles recognized the need for workers who would assist in the equitable distribution of food (there had been accusations of partiality and neglect in this area). The apostles also articulated certain qualifications that were necessary when they gave this directive (Acts 6:3, NLT): "...select seven men who are well respected and are full of the Spirit and wisdom. We will give them this responsibility."

The apostles were not simply looking to "unload" work on someone else. It was imperative that those who carried out this assignment of fairly distributing resources met certain qualifications and could handle this responsibility.

- They had to be well respected, trusted, and have a good reputation.

- They had to be full of the Holy Spirit.

- They had to be full of wisdom.

As the gospel spread and churches were established in other nations, Paul provided certain guidelines for those who would serve as deacons.

Likewise deacons must be reverent, not double-tongued, not given to much wine, not greedy for money, holding the mystery of the faith with a pure conscience. But let these also first be tested; then let them serve as deacons, being found blameless. Likewise, their wives must be reverent, not slanderers, temperate, faithful in all things. Let deacons be the husbands of one wife, ruling their children and their own houses well.

1Timothy 3:8-12

As you read these various lists of qualifications, did you notice that most every requirement had to do with character? In all of these situations, godly work was supposed to be carried out by godly people. The traits that are mentioned in these lists (God-fearing, integrity, well-respected, blameless, self-controlled, etc.) are, in reality, simply the characteristics of Christ-like maturity. They are not unattainable "badges of distinction," that are only available to a few specially called individuals. Actually, every Christian, regardless of any specific ministerial assignment, is called to grow in godliness and Christlikeness. The Apostle Peter said:

...make every effort to respond to God's promises. Supplement your faith with a generous provision of moral excellence, and moral excellence with knowledge, and knowledge with self-control, and self-control with patient endurance, and patient endurance with godliness, and godliness with brotherly affection, and brotherly affection with love for everyone.

The more you grow like this, the more productive and useful you will be in your knowledge of our Lord Jesus Christ. But those who fail to develop in this way are shortsighted or blind, forgetting that they have been cleansed from their old sins.

So, dear brothers and sisters, work hard to prove that you really are among those God has called and chosen. Do these things, and you will never fall away. Then God will give you a grand entrance into the eternal Kingdom of our Lord and Savior Jesus Christ.

2 Peter 1:5-11 (NLT)

How are you doing in the following areas?

- Moral Excellence

- Knowledge

- Self-Control

- Patient Endurance

- Godliness

- Brotherly Affection

- Love for Everyone

If development in all of these areas was automatic for Christians, Peter would not have stressed the need for us to grow in these ways, nor would he have mentioned the possibility of some people failing to develop in these areas.

The last thing that I desire for anyone who reads this book is to decide that they are not perfect enough, and give up on the idea of serving God. We need to understand that God is for us! He is not a fault-finding, critical God who is looking for ways to keep us from engaging in Christian service. However, He is seeking to help us become all that He has called us to be so that we can have credibility with others and bring Him glory.

Even young believers who have just recently given their hearts to God can look for opportunities to love and serve others. Sure, there are qualifications that apply, especially to higher ministerial offices and more visible expressions of service, but that doesn't mean that young Christians can't be used of God while they are still growing.

When It Comes to Higher Positions...

When it comes to more visible and influential roles in the church, some growth and development is required. Paul spoke of deacons and said, "Let them be closely examined. If they pass the test, then let them serve as deacons" (1 Timothy 3:10, NLT). Indicating the need for seasoned spiritual leadership, Paul also taught, "An elder must not be a new believer, because he might become proud, and the devil would cause him to fall" (1 Timothy 3:6, NLT). The phrase "new believer" in the Greek literally means "newly planted," and refers to a new or recent convert.[4]

Scripture teaches us that "to whom much is given, from him much will be required; and to whom much has been committed, of him they will ask the more" (Luke 12:48). It is good to get young believers to serve God in "age appropriate" ways, just as it's good for a toddler to learn responsibility by picking up his toys. As a child matures, he will be able to do more and more. Baby Christians should not feel that they can't do anything at all for God; however, they should understand that as they grow in maturity and faithfulness, they will be able to be used in carrying out higher levels of responsibility.

Questions for Reflection and Discussion

1. Moses was at a point of complete overload before his father-in-law instructed him to delegate and enlist others to help him. Why do you think that Moses had not delegated anything up until this time? What are some of the reasons why you think leaders might be reluctant to delegate?

_____

_____

_____

---

[4]Earle, Ralph, *Word Meanings in the New Testament.* (Peabody, MA: Hendrickson Publishers, 1986) 391.

_____

_____

2. Review the list of the four qualifications for those who were selected to help Moses and the three qualifications for those who were chosen to help the apostles. How essential are such traits today, and why would each of these be needful?_____

_____

_____

_____

3. Look at the seven traits that Peter identified for Christian growth and development. Rate how well you are doing in each of these areas. In which of these areas do you feel that you need the most growth?

_____

_____

_____

_____

4. Why would more be expected from a pastor, or another highly visible church leader, than from someone who simply attended church or served in a very basic way?_____

_____

_____

_____

5. What is the main insight that you have gained from this chapter?

_____

_____

_____

_____

_____

Chapter Five

THE DANGER OF DISQUALIFICATION

"If you keep yourself pure, you will be a special utensil for honorable use. Your life will be clean, and you will be ready for the Master to use you for every good work."

-2 Timothy 2:21(NLT)

Key Thought: *Paul wasn't just concerned about leading and influencing others, but he also saw the great need to make sure that he – himself – was staying on track. If you are playing to win, you have to play by the rules.*

The Apostle Paul recognized that the journey of spiritual leadership is challenging, and that great diligence is required to finish well. Likening the Christian journey to a track race, he said:

Don't you realize that in a race everyone runs, but only one person gets the prize? So run to win! All athletes are disciplined in their training. They do it to win a prize that will fade away, but we do it for an eternal prize. So I run with purpose in every step. I am not just shadowboxing. I discipline my body like an athlete, training it to do what it should. Otherwise, I fear that after preaching to others I myself might be disqualified.

1 Corinthians 9:24-27 (NLT)

In my early Christian experience, I found Paul's statement alarming: I fear that after preaching to others I myself might be disqualified. What would it mean to become "disqualified"? When I first began reading the Bible, the King James rendering of that verse was even more unsettling, as Paul expressed a desire not to end up as a "castaway." Later, as a Bible school student and an aspiring young minister, I heard sober warnings of ministers who ended up on the proverbial "spiritual junk-heap" because of flagrant disobedience and persistent unfaithfulness. Sadly, I have also seen some end up that way.

However, in this statement, Paul is not speaking of sonship; he is speaking of effective, enduring ministry that is carried out without self-inflicted implosions. He is referring to being a spiritual athlete who is exerting great effort, not for personal glory, but for kingdom advancement. Paul uses sports terminology to introduce the idea of potential disqualification. He speaks of athletic rigors and the discipline necessary to be proficient and fruitful in ministry.

Notice that Paul wasn't just concerned about "preaching to others." He was diligent to discipline his own body, and as the NKJV says, "bring it into subjection." Paul realized that before he could lead others, he first had to lead himself. Before he could effectively influence others, he first had to influence himself to stay "on-course." It is terribly unfortunate when ministers seek to excel in their public performance, but deteriorate in their character and integrity. Patsy Cameneti once remarked, "In the process of becoming great preachers, some become lousy Christians."

The easiest thing that you will ever do in ministry is stand behind a pulpit and tell someone else how they are supposed to live and what they are supposed to do. Our challenge is not just in being a proclaimer of the Word, but in being a doer of the Word. "Doing" lends great authenticity to our teaching.

George Whitfield was once asked if a certain individual was a good man. He wisely responded, "How should I know that? I never lived with him." God does not judge our spirituality or godliness based on how we preach or by how we act when people we want to impress are watching. It's not that how we act in public or at church is unimportant, but I believe the ultimate test of spirituality is how we act at home with our spouse and our children, and how we act when no one is watching.

In the first chapter, we discussed the selection of David when he was chosen to be the new king of Israel. That section of Scripture also deals with the rejection of Saul as the "self-disqualified" king of Israel.

And Samuel said to Saul, "You have done foolishly. You have not kept the commandment of the LORD your God, which He commanded you. For now the LORD would have established your kingdom over Israel forever. But now your kingdom shall not continue. The LORD has sought for Himself a man after His own heart, and the LORD has commanded him to be commander over His people, because you have not kept what the LORD commanded you."

1 Samuel 13:13-14

Later, in 1 Samuel 15:23, Samuel said to Saul, "Because you have rejected the word of the LORD, He also has rejected you from being king."

The Apostle Paul's Hebrew name was also Saul, and he was from the same tribe (Benjamin) as King Saul from the Old Testament. He had been named after this disobedient king, who had disqualified himself from Kingdom leadership. Paul was determined not to follow in the same footsteps of disobedience and disqualification as his namesake. Instead, Paul had resolved to finish his course with joy (Acts 20:24).

Since Paul used a sporting event (track) to illustrate his point, perhaps we can glean more insight by exploring this topic also. In track, a sprinter who "false starts" or gets out of his lane, may be disqualified from that particular event. However, this doesn't mean that he is banned from track forever. For this particular race though, he has to step aside and let other runners run without him.

Diego Mesa is a friend of mine who pastors a church in southern California. He used to run marathons and participate in triathlons. In the early 1980's, he felt great as he finished third in a very competitive event. He had done well in the swimming, cycling, and running events, so he happily went to collect his prize of $250 (that was a lot of money to him back then). However, instead, he received a check for $175 and was informed that he had neglected to wear his helmet during the cycling portion of the event. As a result, $75 had been deducted from his award. I wonder how many believers, and even preachers, will stand before the Lord, thinking that they have done wonderful things for Him, only to find out their reward had been affected by wrong motives, attitudes, or methods.

Paul advised Timothy, a young pastor, "...athletes cannot win the prize unless they follow the rules" (2 Timothy 2:5, NLT). In trying to avoid legalism, many have downplayed the idea of "rules," however, there are definite guidelines and principles involved in carrying out fruitful and effective ministerial service. Likewise, ignoring or violating such axioms and precepts can diminish one's productivity greatly, and ultimately affect their reward.

Jesus spoke plainly about a person's spiritual influence being diminished or completely destroyed. "Let me tell you why you are here. You're here to be salt-seasoning that brings out the God-flavors of this earth. If you lose your saltiness, how will people taste godliness? You've lost your usefulness and will end up in the garbage" (Matthew 5:13, MSG).

It was in this same vein of thought that Paul expressed concern that if he did not conduct his life in a godly manner, he might lose his usefulness and become disqualified. In speaking to one group of believers, Paul said, "Examine yourselves as to whether you are in the faith. Test yourselves. Do you not know yourselves, that Jesus Christ is in you?—unless indeed you are disqualified. But I trust that you will know that we are not disqualified" (2 Corinthians 13:5-6).

In order to become disqualified, it seems that a person would have to become qualified in the first place. Speaking of his own ministry, Paul said, "God tested us thoroughly to make sure we were qualified to be trusted with this Message" (1 Thessalonians 2:3, MSG).

So What Do We Do?

Our task is to whole-heartedly pursue those characteristics that qualify us for effective service, and eradicate those traits from our lives that would disqualify us. Paul's analogy and admonition in 2 Timothy 2:20-21 (NLT) supports this entirely.

In a wealthy home some utensils are made of gold and silver, and some are made of wood and clay. The expensive utensils are used for special occasions, and the cheap ones are for everyday use. If you keep yourself pure, you will be a special utensil for honorable use. Your life will be clean, and you will be ready for the Master to use you for every good work.

Questions for Reflection and Discussion

1. Review the main text for this chapter (1 Corinthians 9:24-27). How have you seen this text in the past? Do you see it any differently now? What does this passage challenge you to focus on and do?_____

_____

_____

_____

_____

_____

2. What does the concept mean to you, "Before you can lead others, you first of all have to lead yourself"?_____

_____

_____

_____

_____

3. Have you ever felt like you "disqualified" yourself from effective service in any way? Do you believe it's possible for a person to become "re-qualified," and if so, what might that process look like?_____

_____

_____

_____

_____

_____

4. In what way does being a "doer of the Word" lend credibility to our words?_____

_____

_____

_____

_____

5. What is the main insight that you have gained from this chapter?

_____

_____

_____

_____

_____

Chapter Six

IS IT LIVE,
OR IS IT MEMOREX?

"For me 'twas not the truth you taught, to you so clear to me so dim. But when you came to me you brought, a sense of Him."
- Beatrice Clelland, "Potrait of a Christian"

Key Thought: *We are called to reflect the character of Christ, but we should never evade our responsibilities by expecting God to do the very things He told us to do.*

I remember a decades-old television commercial from Memorex, a company that made audio-cassette tapes. A glass was shown sitting on a table, while the voice of Ella Fitzgerald was heard singing. When a certain high note was hit, the glass shattered and the viewer was asked, "Is it live, or is it Memorex?" The point is that the quality of their product was so high that taped recordings were essentially indistinguishable from the live voice.

This makes me wonder what kind of "reproduction quality" is happening in our lives. Is it possible for us to be so infused with, and transformed by God's Spirit, that what comes out of us remarkably reflects God's very nature?

If you stop and think about it, our life is supposed to be a duplication, of sorts, of the Lord Jesus Christ.

- Luke 6:40 says, *"A disciple is not above his teacher, but everyone who is perfectly trained will be like his teacher."*

- Ephesians 5:1 in the Amplified reads, *"Therefore be imitators of God [copy Him and follow His example], as well-beloved children [imitate their father]."*

- *"He who says he abides in Him ought himself also to walk just as He walked"* (1 John 2:6).

When Jesus called His disciples, His initial priority was not for them to go out and preach; His first priority was for them to be *with Him* (see Mark 3:13-15). Jesus knew that the personal transformation that they would receive through relationship and fellowship with Him, was foundational to their future work in ministry. In other words, Jesus placed the primary emphasis on who they would *become*, not simply on what they would ultimately *do*.

It was through their time with Jesus that the disciples learned His attitudes, values, and priorities. Here are just a few of the values that they received from their association with Jesus:

- They learned that they were not supposed to be in competition and strife with one another (Matthew 20:20-26).

- They learned that they should not have attitudes that were territorial and exclusive regarding ministry (Mark 9:38-39).

- They learned that Jesus did not see children as a nuisance to be shunned, but as honored members of God's family (Mark 10:13-16).

- They learned that revenge was not an appropriate response to those who did not receive Jesus' ministry (Luke 9:51-55).

- They learned it was right to fulfill their civil obligations (Matthew 17:24-26; 22:17-22).

The Spirit of God had worked so deeply and profoundly in the life of the Apostle Paul, that he seemed to wrestle at times with the question, "Is this me, or is it God in me?"

I am crucified with Christ: nevertheless I live; yet not I, but Christ liveth in me...

Galatians 2:20 (KJV)

I laboured more abundantly than they all: yet not I, but the grace of God which was with me.

1 Corinthians 15:10

What a delightful dilemma! The indwelling work of the Holy Spirit within Paul's human spirit was such that he said, "I live" or "I worked," but then he would have to clarify and say, "...but it really wasn't me... at least it certainly wasn't just me; it was Christ living and working through me."

Paul did not believe that Christ dwelling in him meant that he had been thrown into a state of passivity, inactivity, or irresponsibility. Certainly he rested in the finished work of Christ, recognizing that God was the source of all life and power within him, but he also recognized that he was an active participant with God. He recognized his complete dependence upon God, but he also recognized that God desired his active cooperation and involvement in serving, obeying, and fulfilling Heaven's plan for his life.

For example, Paul said in Colossians 1:29 (Amplified), "For this I labor [unto weariness], striving with all the superhuman energy which He so mightily enkindles and works within me." So back to an earlier question

—Was this Paul, or was this God? I don't think we can answer that as an "either/or;" I think it is clearly a "both/and." It was God working in and through Paul, AND it was Paul yielding to and cooperating with God.

Don't Expect God to Do What He Told You to Do

We need to accurately discern what God's role is in our lives, and what our role is; what are His responsibilities and what are our responsibilities? If people simply think that God is going to do everything, they can slip into a sense of irresponsibility and passivity. On the other hand, if people think that they are going to do it all (without the empowerment and enablement of God), they are going to end up worn out, frustrated, and exhausted.

Paul did not say, "I don't live at all; it's all Christ." Neither did he say, "I didn't do any work of any kind, it was only God's grace doing it all." Paul said, "Nevertheless, I live..." and "I labored more abundantly than they all..." He qualified his role, though, by recognizing God as the Source of his life and his labors.

One individual read Romans 8:26 ("...the Spirit Himself makes intercession for us...") and said that he had quit praying and was just letting the Holy Spirit do all of his praying for him. No, we can't expect God to do what He's clearly told us to do, but we can trust Him to help and empower us as we obey Him.

What About Works?

Ephesians 2:9 and Titus 3:5 emphatically state that our salvation is NOT based on our works! The gift of salvation is God's part. He offers that to us freely, based on the finished work of Christ, and we receive His wonderful gift by faith. However, if you read just a bit further, Ephesians

2:10 and Titus 3:8 say that we are saved for good works, and that we are also supposed to maintain these good works. That is our part!

Together, salvation by grace through faith AND good works that result from and follow that salvation, point us toward the whole counsel of God. This does not present a contradiction; but rather, a progression. Salvation, of course, starts with God saving us when we were completely incapable of saving ourselves. However, once He has saved us and made us His children through faith, He works in us to the degree that we see Philippians 2:13 (AMP) becoming a reality in our lives: "Not in your own strength] for it is God Who is all the while effectually at work in you [energizing and creating in you the power and desire], both to will and to work for His good pleasure and satisfaction and delight."

Is this you, or is this God? It is neither you nor God exclusively. It is God "working" in you, and it is you "yielding" yourself in submission and obedience to God. The verse that precedes this statement tells believers to, "work out your own salvation with fear and trembling" (Philippians 2:12). Notice that Paul did not say to work for your salvation, but rather, to work it out. The Amplified renders verse 12, "...work out (cultivate, carry out to the goal, and fully complete) your own salvation with reverence and awe and trembling..."

We are seated with Christ in heavenly places (Ephesians 2:6), but we also have to walk in this world (Ephesians 4:1) and stand against spiritual wickedness (Ephesians 6:10). Being "seated" means that we are supposed to rest in the finished work of Christ. "Walking" and "standing" means that we are supposed to act on the finished work of Christ.

What About Cleansing?

Does God cleanse us or do we cleanse ourselves? Every Christian I know would heartily rejoice in the fact that God, through the blood of the

Lord Jesus Christ, has cleansed us from all sin! As a matter of fact, we read of this great truth in Hebrews 9:14: "...how much more shall the blood of Christ, who through the eternal Spirit offered Himself without spot to God, cleanse your conscience from dead works to serve the living God?"

While Hebrews 9:14 stresses God's part in our cleansing, various other Scriptures emphasize our responsibility in cooperating with and obeying God in the overall process of living a holy life here on earth. Second Corinthians 7:1 says, "Therefore, having these promises, beloved, let us cleanse ourselves from all filthiness of the flesh and spirit, perfecting holiness in the fear of God."

Someone might say, "Wait a minute! If God cleanses us, then how do we cleanse ourselves? Wouldn't that be unnecessary?" That's a very logical question, but we need to understand that these types of Scriptures are not contradictory; they are complementary. There is a "God-ward" side of our redemption (what He did for us), and a "man-ward" side (how we respond to and act upon what He did).

The book of Ephesians illustrates this perfectly. Chapters 1-3 can be summed up in a single word: "Done." Those first three chapters of Ephesians emphasize what Christ has done for us. In these chapters, we find that we have been "blessed with every spiritual blessing in heavenly places" (1:3), have been "accepted in the beloved" (1:6), and that we are seated with Christ in heavenly places (2:6). All of this speaks of what He has already done for us and *in* us.

But Paul doesn't stop with "Done." In Ephesians 4-6, he proceeds to instruct believers about "Do." He addresses what we are to do, and how we are to live in the light of what Christ has done for us. The Bible doesn't just teach about the spiritual life we have from Christ, but it also teaches us about the practical lifestyle we are to lead because of Christ. Ephesians 4:1 sets the tone for the remainder of the epistle: "I... beseech you to walk worthy of the calling with which you were called..."

Is it God or is it us? The truth is that it is both. God does His part and we do our part. Jude 24 says that God, "...is able to keep you from stumbling" and 1 Peter 1:5 says that we are "kept by the power of God..." God's part is clearly articulated, but as we read other scriptures, we see that we have a part to play as well. John said, "he who has been born of God keeps himself" (1 John 5:18) and also, "Little children, keep yourselves from idols" (1 John 5:21). Jude also instructed believers, "keep yourselves in the love of God" (Jude 21). James even said that a component of pure religion is, "to keep oneself unspotted from the world" (James 1:27).

Paul said that Christ gave Himself for us so that He might, "purify for Himself His own special people" (Titus 2:14). Then he tells Timothy, "keep yourself pure" (1 Timothy 5:22). The Apostle John said, "everyone who has this hope in Him purifies himself, just as He is pure" (1 John 3:3). So, does God purify us, or do we purify ourselves? The answer is a resounding "yes!" We should never think that we can do anything of spiritual or eternal significance, apart from His enablement, assistance, and empowerment, but neither should we think that true discipleship involves a passive, inactive, or disengaged state on our part. The wonderful, finished work of Christ does not nullify our responsibility to be "doers of the Word" (James 1:22). As we trust and follow the Lord Jesus Christ, we actively yield to, obey, and cooperate with His plan and purpose that is being worked out in our lives.

What About Being Qualified?

Just like the above illustrations, there is a "God-part" and a "man-part" in the process of our being qualified. God provides all of the raw materials: His calling, His Spirit, His gifts, and His guidance. We receive these gifts and allow them to influence our lives. He qualifies us, and we walk in that realm of qualification. He does it, but we participate with Him.

Questions for Reflection and Discussion

1. How is the "reproduction quality" in your life? How well are you reflecting the nature of God in your character?_____

_____

_____

_____

_____

2. Why do you think Jesus' initial and top priority for His disciples was that they be with Him, rather than focusing on what they could do for Him?

_____

_____

_____

_____

3. Have you ever had occasion to question whether it was you doing something or if it was God working through you?_____

_____

_____

_____

_____

4. What does the phrase, "work out your own salvation with fear and trembling" mean to you?_____

_____

_____

_____

5. What is the main insight that you have gained from this chapter?_____

_____

_____

_____

Chapter Seven

THE RIGHT
STUFF

"Integrity means that if our private life was suddenly exposed, we'd have no reason to be ashamed or embarrassed. Integrity means that our outward life is consistent with our inner convictions."[5]

- Billy Graham

Key Thought: *Integrity and faithfulness are essential to the foundation of true spiritual leadership.*

There he stood, an old, gray-haired prophet. His countenance reflected a lifetime of service that had been marked with honesty and integrity. Tears may have moistened his eyes as he reflected on his journey over the decades and addressed the ones he had served (1 Samuel 12:2-5 NLT).

"I have served as your leader from the time I was a boy to this very day. Now testify against me in the presence of the LORD and before his anointed one. Whose ox or donkey have I stolen? Have I ever cheated any of you? Have I ever oppressed you? Have I ever taken a bribe and perverted justice? Tell me and I will make right whatever I have done wrong."

[5]Billy Graham. The Journey. Nashville. W Publishing Group. 2006. Page 189.

"No," they replied, "you have never cheated or oppressed us, and you have never taken even a single bribe."

"The LORD and his anointed one are my witnesses today," Samuel declared, "that my hands are clean."

"Yes, he is a witness," they replied.

Samuel had finished his course with clean hands and a clean heart. He had withstood the temptations that all leaders face, and he had refused to forfeit his integrity or give into the lure of exploiting people or abusing his power.

Integrity and Math

The word "integrity" is actually related to a mathematical term, "integer." An integer is a whole number - one that is not divided or does not contain a fraction. For example, 2 and 7 are integers. 3 2/3 or 5.7 are not. A person with integrity, therefore, is one who is not divided; he is a "whole" person. He's not living 92% for God and 8% for the indulgence of sin. He doesn't tell the truth 96% of the time, and exaggerate or tell lies the other 4%. I realize that no human being on this earth is flawlessly perfect or incapable or erring, but a person of integrity is not living a double-life. If he misses it in an area, he repents, receives forgiveness, makes the correction, and continues moving forward. He does not lead a lifestyle that is partly committed to holiness and partly not.

Echoing Samuel's legacy of integrity, Paul said,

- *"Open your hearts to us. We have wronged no one, we have corrupted no one, we have cheated no one"* (2 Corinthians 7:2).

- *"...I myself always strive to have a conscience without offense toward God and men"* (Acts 24:16).

- *"You are witnesses, and God also, how devoutly and justly and blame-lessly we behaved ourselves among you who believe..."* (1 Thessalonians 2:10).

Integrity Influences Others

Paul taught that no matter how high or low our standing in society might be, every follower of the Lord Jesus Christ can be qualified or dis-qualified - effective or ineffective - when it comes to being a positive influence on others. Living in a society where slavery was commonplace, Paul instructed Christian slaves how to be a positive witness:

Slaves must always obey their masters and do their best to please them. They must not talk back or steal, but must show themselves to be entirely trustworthy and good. Then they will make the teaching about God our Savior attractive in every way.

Titus 2:9-10 (NLT)

The point? A person does not need to have a high status in life or a lofty ministerial position to have a positive influence on others. It's not about our status or position; it's ultimately about our character and conduct.

Joseph is a great biblical example of an individual who had the favor of God on his life when he was a slave and a prisoner (and eventually as the Prime Minister of Egypt). He deliberately and intentionally maintained his integrity before God, even when propositioned by Potiphar's wife. Joseph did not self-indulgently exploit the situation, but instead clung tenaciously to the plan and will of God for his life. He said, "How then can I do this great wickedness, and sin against God?" (Genesis 37:9).

Daniel is another outstanding example of a man whose life reflected godly character. Long before he was a prophet, he was a student with strong, godly convictions. After that, he served as Prime Minister of two different empires. His positions, though, did not define him; his character did.

> *Daniel soon proved himself more capable than all the other administrators and high officers. Because of Daniel's great ability, the king made plans to place him over the entire empire. Then the other administrators and high officers began searching for some fault in the way Daniel was handling government affairs, but they couldn't find anything to criticize or condemn. He was faithful, always responsible, and completely trustworthy.*
>
> Daniel 6:3-4 (NLT)

A story of unknown origin has long circulated in sermon illustration books, and now is found widely on the Internet. Whether this story is factual or merely anecdotal, it makes a great point:

> Several years ago, a preacher from out-of-state accepted a call to a church in Houston, Texas.
>
> Some weeks after he arrived, he had an occasion to ride the bus from his home to the downtown area. When he sat down, he discovered that the driver had accidentally given him back a quarter too much change.
>
> As he considered what to do, he thought to himself, *You'd better give the quarter back. It would be wrong to keep it.* Then he thought, *Oh, forget it, it's only a quarter. Who would worry about this little amount? Anyway, the bus company gets too much fare; they will never miss it. Accept it as a 'gift from God' and keep quiet.*
>
> When his stop came, he paused momentarily at the door, and then he handed the quarter to the driver and said, 'Here, you gave me too much change.'
>
> The driver, with a smile, replied, 'Aren't you the new preacher in town?'

'Yes,' he replied.

'Well, I have been thinking a lot lately about going somewhere to worship. I just wanted to see what you would do if I gave you too much change. I'll see you at church on Sunday.'

When the preacher stepped off of the bus, he literally grabbed the nearest light pole, held on, and said, 'Oh God, I almost sold Your Son for a quarter.'

Commenting on the influence of David Livingstone upon his life, Henry M. Stanley said, "When I saw the unwearied patience, that unflagging zeal, those enlightened sons of Africa, I became a Christian at his side, though he never spoke to me one word."

Revealing the power of example, Francis of Assisi reportedly said, "Preach the Gospel at all times and when necessary use words."

As God's ambassadors in the earth, we are not simply called to preach a message, but to lead exemplary lives that, according to Titus 2:10, "... make the teaching about God our Savior attractive in every way."

We would be foolish, though, to think that we are the ones who cause people to come to God. Paul also said, "For we do not preach ourselves, but Christ Jesus the Lord, and ourselves your bondservants for Jesus' sake" (2 Corinthians 4:5). He understood totally that the gospel is the power of God unto salvation (Romans 1:16). Nevertheless, our lives are intended to express the goodness of the gospel to others, not distract them from it.

Integrity Is Connected to Faithfulness

And I thank Christ Jesus our Lord who has enabled me, because He counted me faithful, putting me into the ministry, although I was formerly a blasphemer, a persecutor, and an insolent man; but I obtained mercy because I did it ignorantly in unbelief.

1 Timothy 1:12-13

We know that Paul's ministry had its origin in the calling and the mercy of God, but there was a response on Paul's part that was essential for his initiation into and promotion in the ministry. What was it? God counted Paul faithful.

Faithfulness is so important that Paul said, "...it is [essentially] required of stewards that a man should be found faithful [proving himself worthy of trust]" (1 Corinthians 4:2 AMP). A steward is one who manages the affairs of another, and that's exactly what we do when we serve God. We should faithfully oversee and carry out the work (His work) that He has assigned us to do.

Some of the synonyms and related words for "faithfulness" include: constant, dedicated, devoted, good, loyal, steadfast, steady, dependable, reliable, responsible, solid, tried, trustworthy, unwavering, determined, resolute, enthusiastic, fervent, and passionate.[6] These are all good descriptive words of what God desires to see in our lives as we respond to His call and His word.

Jesus described the essential nature of faithfulness in Luke 16:10-12 (NLT).

> *"If you are faithful in little things, you will be faithful in large ones. But if you are dishonest in little things, you won't be honest with greater responsibilities. And if you are untrustworthy about worldly wealth, who will trust you with the true riches of heaven? And if you are not faithful with other people's things, why should you be trusted with things of your own?"*

There are three distinct areas in our lives where God looks for faithfulness:

1. **In Small Things** (If you are faithful in little things, you will be faithful in large ones.) Some people have the idea that it's okay if they become faithful when God gives them a really big, important assignment. In

---

[6]"faithfulness." Merriam-Webster.com. 2012. http://www.merriam-webster.com(29 May 2012)

the meantime, though, it's okay to give half-hearted or minimal effort to one's current assignment, if it doesn't seem all that big or exciting. On the contrary, Jesus said that it is vital for us to be faithful in even the small things, and that our faithfulness in small things indicates that we would be faithful in larger assignments.

Someone said, "God has no larger field for the man who is not faithfully doing his work where he is."[7]

2. **In Practical or Natural Things** ("...if you are untrustworthy about worldly wealth, who will trust you with the true riches of heaven?") Faithfulness applies to far more than just things that are deemed spiritual or religious. Jesus specifically refers to material wealth and solidly implies that exercising good stewardship toward natural things is a pre-requisite to being trusted with spiritual things. If people are careless or reckless in handling their money, then this is indicative of how they would handle spiritual riches.

3. **In Things that Are Not Your Own** ("...if you are not faithful with other people's things, why should you be trusted with things of your own?") Some express a desire for their "own" ministry, but how well have they done in helping someone else fulfill the assignment that God has given them? The important thing is not that I am in charge, but that God's will is accomplished. If that means taking a supportive role, then we should be just as enthusiastic and committed as if we were the "senior" leader.

---

[7] Kelly, Bob, *Worth Repeating: More Than 5,000 Classic and Contemporary Quotes* (Grand Rapids: Kregel Publications, 2003), 115.

Questions for Reflection and Discussion

1. Review Samuel's amazing testimony of integrity toward the end of his life. What would you like to be able to say about your life and your conduct when you are approaching your finish line?_____

_____

_____

_____

_____

_____

2. Paul talked about making "the teaching about God our Savior attractive in every way." What are your thoughts about that? How does a believer do that, and why is this important?_____

_____

_____

_____

_____

_____

3. What did you think of the story of the bus driver and the quarter? Can you think of other scenarios in which this same type of thing could play out?_____

_____

_____

_____

_____

_____

4. What does faithfulness mean to you in your life? How are you endeavoring to be faithful in small things, in practical things, and in things that are not your own?_____

_____

_____

_____

_____

_____

_____

5. What is the main insight that you have gained from this chapter?

_____

_____

_____

_____

_____

_____

_____

_____

Chapter Eight

THE
WRONG STUFF

"It is of no use for any of you to try to be soul-winners if you are not bearing fruit in your own lives. How can you serve the Lord with your lips if you do not serve Him with your lives? How can you preach His gospel with your tongues, when with hands, feet, and heart you are preaching the devil's gospel, and setting up an antichrist by your practical unholiness?"[8]

- Charles H. Spurgeon

Key Thought: *Bad character distracts from and undermines a great message.*

Not far from Samuel was another leader named Saul. Called by God to be king, he floundered with inconsistency and instability. He was unprincipled, erratic, and arbitrary in his leadership, and unlike Samuel, Saul's legacy is that of disobedience, jealousy, rage, and shame.

What causes one leader to finish his or her course with honor, while another's is finished in dishonor? This is addressed on the following pages.

---

[8]Spurgeon, Charles H., "The Soul Winner." A sermon preached Thursday evening, January 20th, 1876, at the Metropolitan Tabernacle, Newington, London.

Many years ago, I spent time with a pastor who had been involved in an extended affair. In the aftermath of his immorality, his wife and children were suffering, and his church was declining. Significant publicity in the community had made his adultery a full-blown scandal. He seemed a bit bewildered that people didn't just forgive and forget. After all, he reasoned, he had apologized, so why couldn't things just go back to the way they had been?

Unfortunately, this minister was confusing the issue of forgiveness with trust. Of course, forgiveness can and should be extended, however, trust is earned. A flagrant betrayal of trust had occurred, and trust is the currency of ministry. This is why Paul said that a church leader, "...must be a man whose life is above reproach. He must be faithful to his wife. He must exercise self-control, live wisely, and have a good reputation." And, "...people outside the church must speak well of him so that he will not be disgraced and fall into the devil's trap" (1 Timothy 3:2,7 NLT).

I shared with him that God indeed forgives, but in some situations one's ability to minister effectively has, nonetheless, been severely compromised and diminished. I also explained (very kindly) that he had disqualified himself from being able to minister during that season of his life in that particular location. Instead of focusing on public ministry, he really needed to take time to focus on establishing personal wholeness while regaining his spiritual equilibrium. This restoration process included seeking healing and restoration for his relationship with his wife and family.

In a totally unrelated situation, I spoke with a distressed young lady whose father was a pastor. Her father was involved with another woman and she said, "My father is two people – he is one person in the pulpit, but he's an entirely different person at home." Such individuals may be a public success (at least for a while), but they are a private failure.

This whole issue does not just apply to preachers; it applies to anyone God has called to have a positive influence on others. For example, let's say that Joe is a professing Christian and is active in his church. Every Sunday, his neighbors see him with his Bible in his hand, taking his family to church in their car (with Jesus bumper stickers). They also hear his occasional references to his faith in Jesus. God's plan is for Joe's life - not just his words - to be a testimony of God's love and goodness.

However, if Joe's neighbor sees him throwing a tantrum later, cussing at the lawn mower, screaming at his children, and kicking his dog, then his influence will not attract them to God, but will rather repel them. Our example matters! Ralph Waldo Emerson said, "What you are shouts so loudly in my ears I cannot hear what you say."

If Joe had exhibited godly character, then the Holy Spirit could have used that to influence his neighbors positively, but his display of uncontrolled anger had disqualified him from having a positive impact on those around him. What if Joe realized how damaging his behavior was to his witness? What if he offered a heartfelt apology to those that he had offended and then began to exhibit the fruit of the Spirit? Could he re-establish his credibility and positively influence his neighbors? Could he "re-qualify" himself and become a good witness? Very likely. As a matter of fact, his conscientiousness, humility, and willingness to change might make a real impression on them.

Our example has the power to attract or repel others. Paul had little appreciation for self-congratulatory individuals who felt that they were spiritually superior to others. Their haughty attitudes and contrary lifestyles were a major turn-off to those who were outside the faith.

...you boast about your special relationship with him. You know what he wants; you know what is right because you have been taught his law.

*You are convinced that you are a guide for the blind and a light for peo-
ple who are lost in darkness. You think you can instruct the ignorant
and teach children the ways of God. For you are certain that God's law
gives you complete knowledge and truth. Well then, if you teach others,
why don't you teach yourself? You tell others not to steal, but do you steal?
You say it is wrong to commit adultery, but do you commit adultery? You
condemn idolatry, but do you use items stolen from pagan temples? You
are so proud of knowing the law, but you dishonor God by breaking it.
No wonder the Scriptures say, "The Gentiles blaspheme the name of God
because of you."*

Romans 2:17-24 (NLT)

Heavy stuff indeed! Sobering. But we need to realize that our witness
in the world and our influence toward others is vital. As Christians and
spiritual leaders, if our lives get out of line then we can receive forgiveness
and move forward. But what about the effect our behavior has on others? We may recover and get things straightened out, but what about the
"fallout" that results in the lives of others due to our conduct? Will they
recover from the negative influence of our bad example? The seriousness of
this issue is highlighted by what Jesus said:

*"Whoever causes one of these little ones who believe in Me to sin, it would
be better for him if a millstone were hung around his neck, and he were
drowned in the depth of the sea. Woe to the world because of offenses! For
offenses must come, but woe to that man by whom the offense comes!*

Matthew 18:6-7

Recognizing the significance and responsibility that comes with influence, C.S. Lewis said, "It matters enormously if I alienate anyone from
the truth."[9]

---

[9] Lewis, C.S., *The Problem of Pain* (New York: HarperSanFrancisco, 1940), 95.

The Strange Case of Rev. Jekyll and Mr. Hyde

You have probably never heard of "Reverend" Jekyll before. I've taken some poetic license and made a slight adjustment to the title of Robert Louis Stevenson's novel from 1886.

In Stevenson's book, Dr. Henry Jekyll is a seemingly good, polite, decent, and respectable man. An experimental potion designed to purify his good side has the unfortunate effect of magnifying his darker side, which results in the emergence of his alter ego, Edward Hyde. Hyde is evil, monstrous, hateful, and murderous. He is the embodiment of evil. More than 125 years later, when people hear the term, "Jekyll and Hyde," they still think of a person who is radically different in his moral character and behavior from one moment to another.

The reason I changed "Dr. Jekyll" to "Rev. Jekyll," is because I want to look at similar dynamics as it relates to spiritual leaders.

Jesus exposed some Rev. Jekylls when He said to the most religious people of His day, "...you are so careful to clean the outside of the cup and the dish, but inside you are filthy—full of greed and self-indulgence! For you are like whitewashed tombs—beautiful on the outside but filled on the inside with dead people's bones and all sorts of impurity. Outwardly you look like righteous people, but inwardly your hearts are filled with hypocrisy and lawlessness" (Matthew 23:25, 27-28, NLT).

Paul had run-ins with more than one Rev. Jekyll. He said, "I have faced danger from men who claim to be believers but are not" (2 Corinthians 11:26, NLT). In the Message version of 2 Thessalonians 3:2, Paul says, "And pray that we'll be rescued from these scoundrels who are trying to do us in. I'm finding that not all 'believers' are believers." How about you? Have you encountered some 'believers' who weren't really believers? Or if they were, they sure didn't conduct themselves as such.

Duplicity among so-called spiritual leaders is something that has been observed throughout church history.

- Augustine said of certain preachers, "With their doctrine they build, and with their lives they destroy." [10]

- John Bunyan said, "Saint abroad, and a devil at home."[11]

- Charles Spurgeon, known as the Prince of Preachers, said, "It is a terribly easy matter to be a minister of the gospel and a vile hypocrite at the same time."[12]

- In *Lectures to My Students,* Spurgeon said, "We have all heard the story of the man who preached so well and lived so badly, that when he was in the pulpit everybody said he ought never to come out again, and when he was out of it they all declared he never ought to enter it again."[13]

- C.S. Lewis said, "Of all bad men religious bad men are the worst."[14]

As Christian leaders, our primary responsibility is not to put on a good front; it is to be truly transformed. Genuine Christianity is substance-based, not image-based. That's why the Apostle John said, "He who says he abides in Him ought himself also to walk just as He walked" (1 John 2:6). Jesus said, "...the student who is fully trained will become like the teacher" (Luke 6:40, NLT).

They profess to know God, but in works they deny Him, being abominable, disobedient, and disqualified for every good work.

Titus 1:16

---

[10]Spurgeon, C.H., *Lectures to My Students* (Grand Rapids, MI: Zondervan, 1954), 19.
[11]Bunyan, John, *Pilgrim's Progress,* (Peabody, MA: Hendrickson Publishers, 2004), 66.
[12] http://thegracetabernacle.org/quotes/Hypocrisy.htm
[13]Spurgeon, C.H., *Lectures to My Students,* (Grand Rapids, MI: Zondervan, 1954), 17.
[14]Lewis, C.S., *Reflections on the Psalms* (New York: Mariner Books, 1964), 32.

Secrets

In recent years, we've seen vivid examples of secular leaders, high profile sports figures, and even ministers having their world implode, because they were leading a secret life (or double life). Such disclosures not only provide fodder for tabloid news, but they also leave a legacy of shattered trust, and leave the people who respected them reeling in shock, pain, and disillusionment. What causes otherwise intelligent people to think that their toxic secrets will never have consequences or be exposed?

The first deception mankind perpetrated was the misbelief that, "We can keep this a secret." Adam and Eve engaged in the first attempted cover-up when "...they sewed fig leaves together and made themselves coverings" (Genesis 3:7). Hearing God calling them, they still felt guilt and shame and endeavored to hide themselves further among the trees of the garden (Genesis 3:8).

Even Moses thought he could get away with murder, as long as no one saw him do it. Exodus 2:12 (NLT) says, "After looking in all directions to make sure no one was watching, Moses killed the Egyptian and hid the body in the sand." This is a good examination point for our lives: Is there anything that we only do if we think no one is watching, or that we think no one will ever find out?

Other biblical accounts remind us that so-called secrets have a way of remaining not-so-secret:

- Achan (Joshua 7:10-25)

- David (2 Samuel 12:12)

- Gehazi (2 Kings 5:25-27)

- Ananias and Saphira (Acts 5:1-11)

Jesus & Paul on Secret Things
(Good and Bad) Coming to Light

You will note that the following scriptures not only deal with negative things (such as "secret sins" coming to light), but also good things that will later be revealed and rewarded.

> *...there is nothing covered that will not be revealed, and hidden that will not be known.*
>
> Matthew 10:26

> *...there is nothing hidden which will not be revealed, nor has anything been kept secret but that it should come to light.*
>
> Mark 4:22

> *...and your Father who sees in secret will Himself reward you openly.*
>
> Matthew 6:4

> *And this is the message I proclaim—that the day is coming when God, through Christ Jesus, will judge everyone's secret life.*
>
> Romans 2:16 (NLT)

> *So don't make judgments about anyone ahead of time—before the Lord returns. For he will bring our darkest secrets to light and will reveal our private motives. Then God will give to each one whatever praise is due.*
>
> 1 Corinthians 4:5 (NLT)

> *But we have renounced the hidden things of shame...*
>
> 2 Corinthians 4:2

Some men's sins are clearly evident, preceding them to judgment, but those of some men follow later. Likewise, the good works of some are clearly evident, and those that are otherwise cannot be hidden.

1 Timothy 5:24-25

For the word of God is alive and powerful. It is sharper than the sharpest two-edged sword... It exposes our innermost thoughts and desires. Nothing in all creation is hidden from God. Everything is naked and exposed before his eyes, and he is the one to whom we are accountable.

Hebrews 4:12-13 (NLT)

What Do We Make of These Passages?

Does this mean that our past sins - ones which have been confessed, repented of, and forsaken - will be brought up by God and used against us? Not at all! Proverbs 28:13 says, "He who covers his sins will not prosper, but whoever confesses and forsakes them will have mercy." Let's not forget the mercy of God, and let's certainly not forget the blood of Jesus which cleanses us from all sin!

I'm not talking about a sin that is acknowledged and renounced, but rather attitudes and behaviors that are nursed, cultivated, and perpetuated - leading to a so-called "secret" or double-life. One of the greatest challenges and temptations that believers (and especially ministers) face is to become totally focused on their outward appearance, while neglecting the care and health of their "inner-life." Ultimately, our lives and ministries must be based on substance and character, not merely image and reputation. John Maxwell said, "Image is what people think we are. Integrity is what we really are."[15]

---

[15]Maxwell, John, *Developing the Leader Within You*, (Nashville: Thomas Nelson, 2005), 41.

When a leader's life and relationships - his real world - become painful, full of pressure, lacking fulfillment, etc., he can be drawn into what he thinks is a private world, in order to escape from reality. In this alternate (false) reality, he medicates himself through illicit relationships, pornography, drugs, alcohol, etc. A deceptive process typically occurs in which the leader begins to believe that God must somehow be condoning or allowing this behavior because, after all, people continue to be saved and blessed through his preaching, and the church may even continue to grow. Misinterpreting the mercy of God as some kind of "divine permission," they fail to realize that God is simply providing them space to repent (see Revelation 2:21).

In a newspaper article addressing the topic of sex in advertising, a representative for an advertising agency said, "Everyone is looking for fantasy, because reality is so cruel." [16] While there may be some observational accuracy to that statement, we must ask the question, *Is turning to fantasy God's plan for His children?*" It's also true that when people struggle with reality, some turn to drugs and alcohol. Christians are instructed to turn to God and His grace to deal with the challenges of reality.

What Do We Need to Do?

It starts with being brutally honest with ourselves. If we are engaging in any type of behavior that we would not want our spouse, friends, other believers, or the public to know about, then we need to get serious with God and ourselves about the matter. We are kidding ourselves if we think that we have really been concealing anything from God anyway.

---

[16]Horowitz, Bruce, "Superbowl Ads Get Racier, but Does Sex Really Sell?" *USA Today,* January 20-22, 2012. http://www.usatoday.com/money/advertising/story/2012-01-19/godaddy-sexy-super-bowl-ads/52686084/1.

David said:

Search me, O God, and know my heart; test me and know my anxious thoughts. Point out anything in me that offends you, and lead me along the path of everlasting life.

Psalm 139: 23-24 (NLT)

The only "secret life" that we are called to have is one with God, not from Him. Psalm 31:20 refers to, "...the secret place of Your presence." Psalm 91:1 tells us that the person who, "...dwells in the secret place of the Most High shall abide under the shadow of the Almighty." May we be ever mindful of the penetrating truth of Hebrews 4:13 (AMP), "And not a creature exists that is concealed from His sight, but all things are open and exposed, naked and defenseless to the eyes of Him with Whom we have to do."

In some cases, accountability to a trusted person can be most helpful. Paul Tournier said, "Nothing makes us so lonely as our secrets." James advocated establishing a godly partnership in overcoming certain issues when he said, "Confess your sins to each other and pray for each other so that you may be healed" (James 5:16, NLT).

As representatives of the Lord Jesus Christ, may it never be said of us what Peter said of false teachers in his day, "They promise freedom, but they themselves are slaves of sin and corruption. For you are a slave to whatever controls you" (2 Peter 2:19, NLT).

Remember that God is for us, not against us, and He wants to help us to become everything He intends for us to be. He doesn't just care about our outward performance, but He cares deeply for the health and well-being of our soul.

Questions for Reflection and Discussion

1. What do you think of the following two phrases?

• Trust is earned._____

_____

_____

_____

_____

_____

• Trust is the currency of ministry._____

_____

_____

_____

_____

_____

2. What types of things would be involved in getting "re-qualified," if a person had become disqualified? Would it always be the same, or would it differ from situation to situation?_____

_____

_____

_____

3. As you read the passage in Romans 2:14-17, were there any areas that you were reminded of where you had taught others one thing, but did not do it yourself?_____

_____

_____

_____

4. This statement was made in this chapter, "The only 'secret life' we are called to have is one with God, not from Him." How well do you feel that is being lived out in your life?_____

_____

_____

_____

_____

_____

5. What is the main insight that you have gained from this chapter?_____

_____

_____

_____

_____

_____

_____

_____

Chapter Nine

YOU ARE
A LETTER

"Out of one hundred men, one will read the Bible, the other ninety-nine will read the Christian."

- D.L. Moody

Key Thought: *Our lives are a letter that others read.*

aul told the Corinthians, "Your very lives are a letter that anyone can read by just looking at you. Christ himself wrote it—not with ink, but with God's living Spirit; not chiseled into stone, but carved into human lives..." (2 Corinthians 3:2-3, MSG).

In addition to the message that we send to the world by our lifestyle and conduct, we need to be aware of how supposedly mature Christians and spiritual leaders influence younger Christians and those who may be weak in the faith.

Paul spent a substantial amount of time (see 1 Corinthians 8 and Romans 14) persuading those who considered themselves to be mature believers to never allow their liberty in Christ to become a stumbling block to those who are less mature or have a weak conscience.

"Therefore, if food makes my brother stumble, I will never again eat meat, lest I make my brother stumble" (1 Corinthians 8:13). Likewise, Paul said, "...if another believer is distressed by what you eat, you are not acting in love if you eat it. Don't let your eating ruin someone for whom Christ died" and, "It is better not to eat meat or drink wine or do anything else if it might cause another believer to stumble" (Romans 14:15, 21 NLT).

Although this context of eating foods that have been sacrificed to idols may be far removed from us historically, however, the principle stands clear. If something we do hinders the faith of another, then we should avoid it.

If the actions of Christians can offend those who are less mature in the faith, it stands to reason that our actions can also influence - negatively or positively - those who are "outside the faith." Tim Tebow, an outspoken Christian and NFL quarterback, was asked if he drank alcohol. His response was, "The biggest reason I don't (consume alcohol) is because (if I have) a glass of wine, I don't want to be responsible for a kid looking up to me and saying, 'Hey Tebow's doing it - I am going to do it.' And then he makes a bad decision. Because like it or not, it's serious," he says.[17]

With this in mind, let's look at three essential truths to understanding our witness in the world.

1. The World Does Not Judge Spiritual Leaders by "Positional" Truth.

One of the most joyous and liberating moments in the lives of believers is when they realize who God has made and declared them to be. Because of the redemptive work of the Lord Jesus Christ, every believer has been declared by God to be:

---

[17]Saraceno, Jon, "Tebow: The Man Behind the Mania," USA Today, January 13-15, 2012. http://www.usatoday.com/sports/football/nfl/story/2012-01-11/tebow-exclusive/52518122/1.

- A child of God (Romans 8:16).

- A new creation (2 Corinthians 5:17).

- The righteousness of God in Christ (2 Corinthians 5:21).

- Blessed with every spiritual blessing in heavenly places in Christ (Ephesians 1:3).

- Accepted in the Beloved (Ephesians 1:6).

- Seated with Christ in heavenly places (Ephesians 2:6).

As wonderful as these insights are to the enlightened believer, the unbeliever has no perception of such truths. The world cannot see our position in Christ; all they can see is what we practice. They cannot see our "eternal life" from Christ; all they can see is our lifestyle.

2. The World Judges Spiritual Leaders by Stricter Standards than Others.

James 3:1 says, "My brethren, let not many of you become teachers, knowing that we shall receive a stricter judgment."

It is simply a fact that people tend to expect more from those in positions of spiritual leadership. In some ways, this may seem unfair and some in ministry get under pressure by always being concerned about what other people are going to think of everything they do and say. For example, some ministry leaders have put enormous pressure on their children to be "perfect" at all times, and in doing so, they allowed the fear of other people and their opinions to have an unhealthy intrusion into their lives.

On the flip side of this, this is a good opportunity to remind church members to remember that pastors and their families are 100% human. Yes, we look to the pastor as a leader and as an example, but keep in mind that they are growing themselves, and there are no doubt, some areas in which their imperfections show up from time to time.

As a young assistant pastor in the early 1980's, my senior pastor had a plaque on his wall with a poem that impressed me. It was entitled, I Am Your Pastor, and this is what it said:

Memo to: My Congregation

From: Your Pastor

When you rise to your highest and best, I am your Pastor.
When you yield to temptation and fall to your lowest,
I am your Pastor.
When you live in the Spirit and manifest the attitude of a
Christian, I am your Pastor.
When for a time you sink to the level of the flesh,
I am your Pastor.
When you walk in the pathway of duty and do God's will,
I am your Pastor.
When you enter the path of disobedience, I am your Pastor.
When joys come to you that swell the notes of praise in your
heart, I am your Pastor.
And when sorrow comes as a dark shroud over your life,
I am your Pastor.
When you have done your best and deserve the approbation of
others, I am your Pastor.
When you have done your best and your good is spoken of as
evil, I am your Pastor.
When you have all you need and more of the necessities of life,
I am your Pastor.
When you feel the pinch of poverty and your power to earn
decreases, I am your Pastor.
When you remain sweet and gracious, as a mature Christian
ought, I am your Pastor.
When you act childish over some real or imagined wrong,
I am your Pastor.

When everything goes right and you have not a care in the
world, I am your Pastor.
When nothing seems right and burdens multiply,
I am your Pastor.
When you please me by the stand you take and the wonderful
spirit you manifest, I am your Pastor.
When you disappoint me and cause me sleepless nights,
I am your Pastor.
When you are living life to the fullest, I am your Pastor.
When your health fails and the end of mortal life seems near,
I am your Pastor.
When I reveal that I am human and have my own weaknesses
and infirmities, and you are charitable and understanding,
I count it a privilege to be your Pastor.

Spiritual leaders will typically find people far more forgiving if they have been compassionate toward others when they have failed and if they do not carry themselves with a haughty, "holier-than-thou" attitude.

Without being overly self-deprecating, it tends to help congregations if their pastor can honestly and humbly acknowledge, with the Apostle Paul, "I don't mean to say that I have already achieved these things or that I have already reached perfection. But I press on to possess that perfection for which Christ Jesus first possessed me. No, dear brothers and sisters, I have not achieved it, but I focus on this one thing: Forgetting the past and looking forward to what lies ahead…" (Philippians 3:12-13, NLT).

It is one thing to humbly, and in the fear of God, invite others, "Imitate me, just as I also imitate Christ" (1 Corinthians 11:1). That's a good thing. It is another thing to arrogantly present oneself as "THE Standard of Perfection" for all others. That is not a good thing.

We should never take ourselves so seriously that we are devastated by criticism. George Whitfield once received a letter of harsh criticism. He responded, "I thank you heartily for your letter. As for what you and my other enemies are saying against me, I know worse things about myself than you will ever say about me. With love in Christ, George Whitfield."

Having said all this, those in spiritual leadership should be aware that people are watching their example to see if their lives are genuine and wholesome. They should also realize - as James said nearly 2,000 years ago - that teachers will be judged more strictly than others.

3. The World Will Form Their Opinion About Jesus, the Bible, and the Church, Not So Much By Our Preaching, but by Our Ethics, Morality, and Conduct.

It has been said, "You are the only Jesus some people will ever see; you are the only Bible some people will ever read."

Ambedkar (1891-1956) was born into an "untouchable" family in the old caste system of India. In spite of the intense discrimination he faced, he obtained an excellent education and became an influential leader in India, even to the point of serving as Chairman on the Drafting Committee of the *Indian Constitution*.

> "When I read the Gospels, the Acts of the Apostles and certain passages of St. Paul's epistles I feel that I and my people must all become Christians, for in them I find a perfect antidote to the poison Hinduism has injected into our souls and a dynamic strong enough to lift us out of our present degraded position; but when I look at the Church produced by Christian Missions in the districts around Bombay I have quite a different feeling. Many members of my own caste have become Christians and most of them do not commend Christianity to the rest of us. Some have gone to boarding schools and have enjoyed high privilege. We think of them as finished products of your missionary effort, and what sort

of people are they? Selfish and self-centered. They do not care a snap of their finger what becomes of their former caste associates so long as they and their families, or they and the little group who have become Christians get ahead. Indeed their chief concern with reference to their old caste associates is to hide the fact that they were ever in the same community. I don't want to add to the number of such Christians." [18]

Likewise, Mohandas Ghandi said, "I like your Christ, I do not like your Christians. Your Christians are so unlike your Christ." He also remarked, "If Christians would really live according to the teachings of Christ, as found in the Bible, all of India would be Christian today."

We don't need to be under condemnation about observations that others have made about our lives in the past, but we should be challenged to be the kind of letter that clearly articulates and makes known the wonders of our God and the virtues of His glorious gospel. May it be so!

Questions for Reflection and Discussion

1. Have you ever shared the Gospel with someone, only to have them put up resistance, citing hypocrisy of certain religious leaders as an excuse? How did you respond?_____

_____

_____

_____

_____

_____

_____

---

[18] McGavran, Donald A. *Understanding Church Growth*, (Grand Rapids, MI: William B. Eerdman's Publishing Company, 1970), 339.

2. Have you ever acted badly in front of unbelievers or young Christians who were taking note of your example? Did you do anything to rectify the situation? What was the result?_____

_____

_____

_____

_____

_____

3. The statement was made, "You are the only Jesus some people will ever see; you are the only Bible some people will ever read." How should that affect the attitude and conduct of a Christian?_____

_____

_____

_____

_____

_____

_____

4. What is the main insight that you have gained from this chapter?

_____

_____

_____

_____

_____

_____

_____

Chapter Ten

INTENTIONAL
INTEGRITY

"Principle - particularly moral principle - can never be a weather vane, spinning around this way and that with the shifting winds of expediency. Moral principle is a compass forever fixed and forever true..."

-Edward R Lyman

Key Thought: *Integrity does not happen by accident. Godly character is established deliberately and intentionally.*

In Psalm 37 and 73, the writer expresses frustration from seeing unethical and crooked people "get ahead," even though they had cut corners and compromised, while the righteous didn't seem to be making as much progress. Psalm 73:13 (MSG) says, "I've been stupid to play by the rules; what has it gotten me? The truth is though, that it's only those who play by God's rules who are going to be standing in the end." After a burst of initial vexation, the psalmist comes to his senses and acknowledges that integrity will remain solid in the end, when every deceitful way has been upended.

Benjamin Disraeli said, "Principle is ever my motto, not expediency." Expedience refers to pursuing whatever is immediately advantageous or personally desirable, without a view toward the ethics, morality, or principle involved in the matter. In contrast, a principled person - one who lives with intentional integrity - is one who embraces a high code of values, and then consistently lives out those values.

Henry Ward Beecher said, "Expedients are for the hour, but principles are for the ages. Just because the rains descend, and the winds blow, we cannot afford to build on shifting sands."[19] When you see people cutting corners and compromising to get quick results or immediate gratification, don't feel that your integrity is in vain. Realize that you are building on a solid foundation—one that will endure and remain over time.

The idea of pragmatism is closely related to expedience. Pragmatism involves a very practical, "whatever works" approach to life. In other words, the validity or value of an idea is determined by the results it produces. While that may sound good (and it is often fine in practical matters), it is not a biblical approach in relation to morals, ethics, and "ultimate truth," as found in the Scriptures. Pragmatism without morals will cause people to think:

- It's okay to hedge on the truth if it allows me to stay out of trouble or achieve my goals.

- It's okay if I show favoritism if it works to my advantage.

- There's no problem with me having an extra-marital affair if it makes me happier in life.

- It's okay not to preach the whole counsel of God's Word if it makes me more popular or gets more people to come to my church.

---

[19]Goodman, Ted, Editor. *The Forbes Book of Business Quotations,* (New York: Black Dog & Leventhal Publishers, 1997), 684.

Godliness is inconsistent with an "ends-justifies-the-means" mentality. Once a person starts down a road of compromise, dishonesty, and duplicity, he will become more calloused to the truth and begin to justify and rationalize all kinds of behaviors, even those he would have previously found completely unacceptable.

Oswald Sanders masterfully describes Paul's unwavering commitment to principle: "Where principle was clearly at stake Paul was inflexible and would not yield for a moment, even if the person involved was the prestigious apostle Peter. Because the vastly important issue of Christian liberty was at issue, Paul told the Galatians, 'We did not give in to them for a moment, so that the truth of the gospel might remain with you' (Galatians 2:5). But when only a preference and not a principle was involved, he was prepared to make large concessions."[20]

Another individual who delineated between the "non-negotiables" (matters of principle and core-values) and "negotiables" was Thomas Jefferson. He said, "In matters of style, swim with the current. In matters of principle, stand like a rock."

In examining the lives of honorable men and women throughout church history, we find that they possessed strong values and convictions. These were not vague, floating aspirations, but they had consciously identified their values and had often articulated them as well.

One spiritual leader who clearly articulated his values was Jonathan Edwards. His verbiage reflects his era, but he certainly embraced and expressed great commitments and principles, such as:

- Resolved, never to do anything out of revenge.

- Resolved, that I will live so as I shall wish I had done when I come to die.

---

[20]Sanders, Oswald, *Dynamic Spiritual Leadership*, (Grand Rapids, MI: Discovery House Publishers, 1999), 16.

- Whenever I hear anything spoken in conversation of any person, if I think it would be praiseworthy in me, Resolved to endeavor to imitate it.

- Resolved, never to give over, nor in the least to slacken my fight with my corruptions, however unsuccessful I may be.

John G. Lake wrote what he called, "My Consecration as a Christian." One of his values was expressed this way: "I will always strive to be a peacemaker. First, by being peaceful myself and avoiding all unfruitful contentions, and treating all with justice and regarding their rights and their free agency, never trying to force any to my point of view. If I should offend anyone knowingly, I shall immediately apologize. I will not scatter evil reports about any person, and so try to defame their character, or repeat things that I am not certain of being true. I will strive to remove the curse of strife among the brethren by acting as a peacemaker."[21]

Men and women don't become great by accident. They are carried into greatness by great values, great decisions, great convictions, great principles, and great actions. One person said, "Make your decisions, and your decisions will make you."

- Make it your determined effort not to grow lax or sloppy in your morals, values, and convictions, even if others around you seem to do so.

- Don't let yourself simply "go with the crowd" when their values or morals are lacking.

- Embrace the highest and the best that God has for you.

- Don't let His Word be a book of ideals from which you can selectively and occasionally live, but let them be your command-

---

[21] Lake, John G., *Adventures in God,* (Tulsa: Harrison House, 1981), 124.

ments—orders given by One in authority about which there is no choice and from which there is no retreat!

Daniel didn't stumble into integrity; the excellence of his character was deliberate and intentional. Daniel 1:8 says, "But Daniel purposed in his heart that he would not defile himself..."

Likewise, Paul was determined to walk in integrity. He said, "I myself always strive to have a conscience without offense toward God and men" (Acts 24:16. The Amplified Bible renders that verse, "I always exercise and discipline myself [mortifying my body, deadening my carnal affections, bodily appetites, and worldly desires, endeavoring in all respects] to have a clear (unshaken, blameless) conscience, void of offense toward God and toward men."

Paul advised the believers to "...take thought for what is honest and proper and noble [aiming to be above reproach] in the sight of everyone" (Romans 12:17, AMP).

In November of 1948, shortly before his ministry was launched into major national prominence, Billy Graham met with three of his top associates (Cliff Barrows, George Beverly Shea, and Grady Wilson) to discuss ways to lead their ministry with integrity and avoid scandalous, shameful practices, which had brought reproach to many in evangelistic-type ministries. In what became known as the "Modesto Manifesto," Graham and his team identified four areas of concern and resolved to conduct themselves with the upmost integrity in these matters.

The four areas that were identified included:

- The shady handling of money

- Sexual immorality

- Badmouthing others doing similar work

- Exaggerated accomplishments

Billy Graham spoke of these guidelines, saying, "In reality, it did not mark a radical departure for us; we had always held these principles. It did, however, settle in our hearts and minds once and for all, the determination that integrity would be the hallmark of both our lives and our ministry." [22]

Here are some decisions that principled leaders have already made:

- To be 100% honest in all of one's dealings.

- To stay completely submitted to the principles of honor and integrity in God's Word.

- To be a good steward of one's body, mind, finances, and gifts.

- If wrong is done, to make it right.

- To be completely faithful to one's spouse, and to maintain moral purity in every way.

- To take the "high road" in all dealings in life.

- To treat all people with dignity and respect.

- To never try to get ahead or make oneself look good by tearing down others.

- To be the best possible example of Christlikeness.

- To never exploit or take advantage of anyone, especially those who are weak and vulnerable.

- To be an authentic person, never putting on a front or facade.

- To always do what is in the best interests of others; seeking their edification and avoiding what will bring harm to others.

[22]Myra, Harold and Shelley, Marshall, *The Leadership Secrets of Billy Graham*, (Grand Rapids: Zondervan, 2005), 57.

Questions for Reflection and Discussion

1. Have you ever felt frustrated when you saw people who were cutting corners and/or doing things wrong, and yet they seemed to prosper and get ahead? How did you handle your frustration, and what did you tell yourself about the situation?_____

_____

_____

_____

_____

_____

_____

_____

2. Thomas Jefferson was quoted as having said, "In matters of style, swim with the current. In matters of principle, stand like a rock." Can you recall yourself implementing that approach in your life? Can you see any area where you might in the future?_____

_____

_____

_____

_____

_____

_____

_____

3. In what specific ways have you determined (like Daniel) that you would not defile yourself? What specific decisions have you made in terms of being holy and pleasing to God?_____

_____

_____

_____

_____

_____

_____

_____

4. Review the list of decisions that principled leaders have already made. How many of those have you intentionally and deliberately decided to implement as a part of your life and your core values?_____

_____

_____

_____

_____

_____

_____

_____

5. What is the main insight that you have gained from this chapter?_____

_____

_____

_____

_____

_____

_____

_____

Chapter Eleven

CULTIVATING COMPETENCE

"Whatever you are, be a good one."

-Abraham Lincoln

Key Thought: *If it's worth doing, it's worth doing right.*

We can never over-estimate the importance of integrity and character, neither should we minimize the significance of being skillful and competent.

Do you remember what Psalm 78:72 said about David? He, "...guided them by the skillfulness of his hands."

If I have a problem with my vehicle, I don't simply want a mechanic who loves Jesus to work on my car; I want a mechanic who is truly skilled in repairing cars. Likewise, if I seek help for a medical condition, I don't just want to see a doctor who is nice and honest; I want a doctor who is highly proficient in accurately diagnosing and treating illnesses.

When it comes to serving God, our desire should be to give Him our absolute best. Even though we realize that our ability ultimately comes from Him, we should endeavor to follow the example of the Lord Jesus Christ. Mark 7:37 (Amplified) says of Jesus: "And they were overwhelmingly astonished, saying, He has done everything excellently (commendably and nobly)…"

Was Jesus a Sloppy Carpenter?

I don't think that Jesus started being committed to quality and excellence when He became a preacher. I believe that His attitude and determination was to do all things to the glory and honor of His Heavenly Father whether that involved making a table as a carpenter or preaching a sermon as a minister.

I just can't imagine Jesus going back to His hometown to preach, and people not being interested in hearing Him because He had been a terrible carpenter. I believe that Jesus did whatever He did to the glory and honor of God. I simply can't see Him as a careless, sloppy, apathetic worker, producing inferior goods.

Throughout the Old Testament, God's appreciation for quality is clearly evident:

- The garments that were made for use in the Old Testament tabernacle were *"skillfully woven"* (Exodus 28:4, 39).

- Those designated to help in building the tabernacle were referred to as *"gifted artisans"* (Exodus 36:1).

- David, before he was ever anointed to be king, was described as, *"…skillful in playing, a mighty man of valor, a man of war, prudent in speech, and a handsome person; and the LORD is with him"* (1 Samuel 16:18).

- In 2 Chronicles 2, Solomon is preparing to build the Temple. In this chapter, he uses the word "skillful" five times and the word "skilled" once.

- Ezra was referred to as a *"skilled scribe"* (Ezra 7:6).

- *"Daniel distinguished himself above the governors and satraps, because an excellent spirit was in him; and the king gave thought to setting him over the whole realm"* (Daniel 6:3).

- Psalm 33:3 says, *"Sing to Him a new song; Play skillfully with a shout of joy."*

- And as a final thought on quality, what is the one thing we all want to hear when we stand before Jesus? *"Well done, good and faithful servant..."* (Matthew 25:21).

Portraits of Excellence

Martin Luther King, Jr. captured the spirit of excellence when he said, "If a man is called to be a street-sweeper he should sweep streets even as Michelangelo painted or Beethoven composed music or Shakespeare wrote poetry. He should sweep streets so well that all the hosts of heaven and earth will pause to say 'Here lived a great street sweeper who did his job well.'" [23]

Aristotle said, "Excellence is an art won by training and habituation. We do not act rightly because we have virtue or excellence, but we rather have those because we acted rightly. We are what we repeatedly do. Excellence, then, is not an act but a habit." [24]

---

[23] Anderson, Peggy, *Great Quotes by Great Leaders,* (Lombard, IL: Celebrating Excellence Publishing, 1990), 11.
[24] Goodman, Ted, *The Forbes Book of Business Quotations,* (New York: Black Dog & Levanthal Publishers, Inc, 1997), 258.

General H. Norman Schwarzkopf shared this observation: "I've met a lot of leaders in the Army who were very competent - but they didn't have character... I've also met a lot of leaders who had superb character but who lacked competence....To lead in the twenty-first century ... you will be required to have both character and competence."[25]

Many have heard of John Wooden, the former basketball coach for UCLA. Perhaps his great achievements were due, at least in part, to the fact that his father taught him when he was young to, "Make each day your masterpiece."

Let's look at some of the areas in which we can develop competence.

Competence in Working with People

Ministry is largely a "people-business." It is great to love God, worship Him, and pray, but we also need to be able to work well with people if we are going to be effective in ministry. Rehoboam is a classic example of a leader, who sabotaged his own effectiveness and potential because he did not know how to establish and maintain good working relationships with people. When the people looked for a little relief from the fatigue that they had experienced under Solomon's reign, Rehoboam answered harshly and roughly. A little kindness and diplomacy would have worked wonders, but Rehoboam lost ten of the twelve tribes, over which he could have ruled (2 Chronicles 10:1-17).

> "The most important single ingredient in the formula of success is knowing how to get along with people."
>
> -Theodore Roosevelt

---

[25]Zuck, Roy B., *The Speaker's Quote Book*, (Grand Rapids: Kregel Publications, 1997), 59.

There are three dimensions of relationships that we need to learn to work with:

- We must work well with those who are in authority over us - the key word here is submission.

- We must work well with those who are our peers and co-workers - the key word here is teamwork. Soccer great Mia Hamm said, "I am a member of a team and I rely on the team, I defer to it and sacrifice for it because the team, not the individual, is the ultimate champion."

- We must work well with those who are under our supervision - the key word here is diplomacy.

The Bible does not say that we are guaranteed automatic success in every relationship, or that we will be able to get along well with every person on earth; however, we should give it our best shot. There are books available that can help us develop our people skills and teach us how to get along with difficult people. We can also learn to bring out the best in others in order to cultivate the best results possible in the various relationships that we have.

Competence in Handling the Word of God

Paul told Timothy, "Be diligent to present yourself approved to God, a worker who does not need to be ashamed, rightly dividing the word of truth" (2 Timothy 2:15). Paul said that a bishop was to be "...a capable and qualified teacher" (1 Timothy 3:2, AMP) and that one serving in such a leadership role must be, "...holding fast the faithful word as he has been taught, that he may be able, by sound doctrine, both to exhort and convict those who contradict" (Titus 1:9).

The competence that we are referring to is not merely having a mental grasp on the truths of Scripture, but it also applies to being spiritually sensitive to the Holy Spirit and the needs of people. Isaiah said, "The Lord GOD has given me the tongue of the learned, that I should know how to speak a word in season to him who is weary. He awakens me morning by morning, He awakens my ear to hear as the learned" (Isaiah 50:4). We don't seek competence in handling Scripture just so we can win arguments, but rather so we will be able to minister effectively to those who are hurting and discouraged.

The Apostle Paul recognized that there was more to competence in ministering the Word of God than being "technically" correct about something, especially if we have a legalistic attitude. He said that God, "...made us sufficient as ministers of the new covenant, not of the letter but of the Spirit; for the letter kills, but the Spirit gives life" (2 Corinthians 3:6). It's important that we not only minister the truth of God, but also the heart of God.

Competence in One's Assigned Area of Responsibilities

This point should be self-evident. If you type letters, then type them well. If you run sound, then excel at it. If you are a greeter, then really make people feel welcome. Whatever you do, do it with the same level of enthusiasm and quality that you would exhibit if you were doing it for Jesus personally.

Dan Reiland said, "Far too often in a church staff environment, we incorrectly apply grace. Someone makes a mistake or falls short of a standard of excellence and we say, 'Ah, that's OK.' It's not OK. Jesus didn't die on the cross for 'OK.' He deserves our best. You can be kind in your communication and patient in your coaching, but don't lower your expectations. The cause of Christ is worth everyone's best."[26]

In many churches, volunteers (and sometimes employees) are chosen to work in an area in which they are not highly competent or proficient. Should they refuse to serve if they don't have a PhD in that area? Certainly not! But they should learn all that they can about that specific area and gain all the proficiency and competence that they can in order to do a good job.

During my first year of Bible school, I worked as a janitor in a local church. I knew how to run a vacuum cleaner, and that was about it. You may be wondering how many mistakes a janitor can make if he's not skilled, well I want you to know that I found out at least some of them!

One of my assignments was to dust the platform area in the sanctuary. As I applied the wax spray and removed the dust, I felt like I was doing a pretty good job. However, it never occurred to me that applying wax spray to the piano keyboard, was not a good idea. Since I was not a musician, I did not realize that piano players did not appreciate slick keys! I was kindly "instructed," and did not make that mistake again.

Employers and supervisors realize that individuals need some training and instruction, and they also assume that an honest mistake will be made from time to time. However, they certainly don't expect people to make the same mistakes over and over again.

In order to be competent and remain competent in our skills, it is imperative that we are teachable - always learning - and always seeking to improve. At times, people are in a certain position, but they don't keep up with new information or the latest technology concerning that position and soon their job "outgrows" them. Someone said, "Don't be yourself. Be superior to the fellow you were yesterday." John Wesley was huge on being a life-long learner. Consider these statements by Wesley:

[26]Reiland, Dan, "Working with a Strong Personality, Part 2," *The Pastor's Coach*, www.Injoy.com.

- "Reading Christians are growing Christians. When Christians cease to read, they cease to grow."

- "He who no longer reads should get out of the ministry."

- "Once in seven years I burn all my sermons; for it is a shame if I cannot write better sermons now than I did seven years ago."

If It's Worth Doing...

We have all heard the phrase. *"If it's worth doing, it's worth doing right."* Oswald Chambers dignified that already great idea through the title of his classic book, *My Utmost for His Highest.* What a beautiful and powerful thought. Ecclesiastes 9:10 (NKJV) also articulated this principle with these words, "Whatever your hand finds to do, do it with your might." Let's apply this to all areas of our lives, especially in our service for God, as we continuously cultivate competence.

Questions for Reflection and Discussion

1. What was the quality of Jesus' work as a carpenter? Why do you think it was that way?_____

_____

_____

_____

_____

_____

_____

_____

2. Review the quote by Martin Luther King, Jr. ("If a man is called to be a street-sweeper...). How much do you see that operating in other people's lives? In your own life?_____

_____

_____

_____

_____

_____

3. It has been stated that we need to get along well with those in authority, with our co-workers, and with those under our supervision. How are you doing in those three areas? Is there one of those that you find the easiest to do? The hardest?_____

_____

_____

_____

_____

_____

4. What is the main insight that you have gained from this chapter?_____

_____

_____

_____

_____

_____

_____

Chapter Twelve

Pitfalls to Avoid in Pursuing Excellence

"Man is the only kind of varmint who sets his own trap, baits it, then steps on it."

- John Steinbeck

Key Thought: *There are substitutes and even counterfeits for excellence. Know them and avoid them.*

There are some who will never encounter certain pitfalls that are associated with pursuing excellence, simply because they never aspire to realize the high quality that God desires. They are not running to win as Paul described in 1 Corinthians 9:24, nor do they "strive for the masteries" as described in 2 Timothy 2:5 (KJV). They may serve God, but only half-heartedly and at the end of their race, they are more likely to hear, *"Well, you're done"* than *"Well done."*

The Pitfall of Mediocrity

Instead of pursuing excellence, some are content with just doing enough to get by. The word *mediocre* comes from two Latin words meaning, "halfway up the mountain." In other words, individuals who operate with a mentality of mediocrity are completely content to do the bare minimum, operate with low standards, and do not care if they achieve maximum results.

What traits will you see when mediocrity prevails?

- An attitude of apathy

- Lack of concern about quality or results

- Contentment with the status quo; no desire for improvement

- No challenging goals

- Tardiness and lack of punctuality; deadlines are not met

- Absence of conscientiousness and diligence

- Sloppiness, carelessness, and a lack of follow-through

- Lack of focus

- Easily succumbs to distractions and diversions

- Low energy levels

- Work is seen as mundane; those involved are simply going through the motions

The Pitfall of Compulsion

You don't get good music out of guitar strings that are too loose; likewise, you don't get good music out of guitar strings that are too tight. Those who are governed by mediocrity lack motivation toward excellence (strings too loose), but those who are compulsive are driven in an unhealthy way (strings too tight).

Compulsive individuals often speak of striving for excellence, but they may be confusing a high regard for quality with hyper-perfectionism. Enjoying high standards and quality outcomes is great, but when a person is continually restless, anxious, and fearful of failure, this is not good. A hyper-perfectionist never feels like anything has been done good enough and is always finding fault. In short, there is no joy in the journey or the destination.

I remember talking with an individual who had a list of 45 things (types of prayers, confessions, things to read, etc.), that he felt like he had to do every morning before he could start his day. While some of these things were good in and of themselves, the way that he approached them was very rigid and legalistic. It was obvious that he had no joy in exercising these spiritual disciplines; they were very burdensome to him.

A person who serves from compulsion probably pictures God being like the harsh taskmasters of Egypt, who were always demanding more (see Exodus 1:7-14; 5:5-14). Instead of seeing Him as the Gentle Shepherd, they see God as angry, disappointed, and always telling them, "You're not praying enough. You're not reading your Bible enough. You're not serving enough, etc." It's important to keep in mind that the Good Shepherd leads His sheep; He doesn't drive them. God leads us with a sense of peace, while the enemy (endeavoring to counterfeit the Holy Spirit) attempts to drive us with a sense of panic.

It's important to remember, that it was Jesus who said, "Come to Me, all you who labor and are heavy laden, and I will give you rest. Take My yoke upon you and learn from Me, for I am gentle and lowly in heart, and you will find rest for your souls. For My yoke is easy and My burden is light" (Matthew 11:28-30).

The Pitfall of Comparison

Comparison is typically based on insecurity and tends to produce either pride or inferiority. Charles Swindoll wisely stated, "Rabbits don't fly. Eagles don't swim. Ducks look funny trying to climb. Squirrels don't have feathers. Stop comparing. Enjoy being you! There's plenty of room in the forest."[27]

When my wife and I finished our first year of Bible school in 1980, we traveled to Australia for the summer to preach in several churches. We began at the church of our primary host who was a prolific Bible teacher. Some of his assistants showed me a filing cabinet that was full of his notes. I was both impressed and intimidated at his volumes upon volumes of teaching outlines.

I was very inexperienced and felt that I needed to come up with a sermon that his congregation would be impressed with. So, I combined three hours worth of class notes that I had taken as a student into one message and thought I had a real masterpiece. However, when I got up to speak, I exhausted my notes in 10-15 minutes, and they were expecting a 50-minute message! I'm not even sure that what I said made much sense. I was inexperienced and had no "filler," so I just stopped. It was very embarrassing, but I learned a couple of valuable lessons:

- Bless people; don't try to impress people.

- Don't try to be someone else.

- Don't try to measure up to someone else's gifts, abilities, or level of experience.

- Just give people what you have to give them, and give it from your heart.

[27]Swindoll, Charles, *Growing Strong in the Seasons of Life*, (Grand Rapids: Zondervan Publishing House, 1983), 342.

David refused to wear Saul's armor; it didn't fit him. David conquered Goliath, not by trying to look like Saul, but by using the tools that he was comfortable with - a sling and some stones. When you copy someone else, you are operating in imitation. Learn to operate by inspiration instead. Inspiration will always be found in doing what God has called you to do - not in mimicking someone else.

Paul deliberately stayed away from comparing himself to others. He said: "Not that we [have the audacity to] venture to class or [even to] compare ourselves with some who exalt and furnish testimonials for themselves! However, when they measure themselves with themselves and compare themselves with one another, they are without understanding and behave unwisely. We, on the other hand, will not boast beyond our legitimate province and proper limit, but will keep within the limits [of our commission which] God has allotted us as our measuring line and which reaches and includes even you" (2 Corinthians 10:12-13, AMP).

God will never judge you based on another person's calling or results. He hasn't called you to be a clone of anyone else or to do what someone else has been assigned to do. Your only objective should be to do the best you can do. Those who fall into the trap of comparison often end up in competition with others as well. Our only competition should be with our own potential - to fully maximize our own gift for the glory of God. Other believers and other churches are our partners, not our competitors.

The disciples had a strong "comparison-competition" issue going, and it continued even after the resurrection. Even when Jesus told Peter, "Follow me," Peter couldn't help but wonder how John's ministry and destiny would compare to his.

Peter turned around and saw behind them the disciple Jesus loved—the one who had leaned over to Jesus during supper and asked, "Lord, who will betray you?" Peter asked Jesus, "What about him, Lord?" Jesus replied, "If I want him to remain alive until I return, what is that to you? As for you, follow me.

John 21:20-22 (NLT)

We need to focus our attention on following Jesus instead of looking around, seeing others, and asking, "What about him, Lord?" If we become overly focused on others, especially with a critical, comparative attitude, then we are likely to begin running others down and feeling like we are in competition with other members of the Body of Christ. We are all on the same team, and we need to respect each others' assignments and cheer them on, as they seek to serve God effectively.

Questions for Reflection and Discussion

1. At the beginning of this chapter, some traits were listed that will show up when mediocrity prevails. Are any of those present in your life? Do you need to make any adjustments?_____

_____

_____

_____

_____

_____

_____

2. Do you relate to God and serve Him from a sense of peace, or do you feel driven?_____

_____

_____

_____

_____

_____

_____

_____

3. What about comparison? Are you secure and at peace with who you are and what you have to offer others? Can you rejoice in other peoples' gifts, without feeling jealous or intimidated?_____

_____

_____

_____

_____

_____

_____

4. What is the main insight that you have gained from this chapter?

_____

_____

_____

_____

_____

_____

_____

_____

_____

MINISTRY KILLERS YOU MUST CONQUER– THE GOLD

Chapter Thirteen

LEADERS ARE TO EMPOWER, NOT EXPLOIT OTHERS

"If a person gets his attitude toward money straightened out, then almost all other areas of his life will be straightened out."

- Billy Graham

Key Thought: *Principled leaders stay free from covetousness and operate in the utmost integrity in all matters pertaining to finances.*

A paramount issue that all leaders must face pertains to whether they will empower or exploit others. Spiritual leaders who are free from covetousness will always seek the welfare and benefit of those to whom they minister. When Paul gave Timothy guidelines for church leaders, much of what he said had to do with the character of leaders relative to their attitudes toward money and how they handled it.

This is a faithful saying: If a man desires the position of a bishop, he desires a good work. A bishop then must be blameless, the husband of one wife, temperate, sober-minded, of good behavior, hospitable, able to teach; not given to wine, not violent, not greedy for money, but gentle, not quarrelsome, not covetous; one who rules his own house well, having his children in submission with all reverence (for if a man does not know how to rule his own house, how will he take care of the church of God?);

not a novice, lest being puffed up with pride he fall into the same con-
demnation as the devil. Moreover he must have a good testimony among
those who are outside, lest he fall into reproach and the snare of the devil.

1 Timothy 3:1-7

Two of the above statements about qualifications for spiritual leaders are direct references to money matters:

- Not greedy for money (verse 3)

- Not covetous (verse 3)

Several other statements have at least an indirect application to money matters:

- Blameless (verse 2)

- Temperate - this means self-controlled (verse 2)

- Sober-minded - this means that one lives wisely (verse 2)

- Of good behavior - this means that one has a good reputation (verse 2)

- Rules (or manages) his own house well (verses 4, 5)

- Takes care of the church of God (verse 5)

- A good testimony of those who are outside (verse 7)

While the majority of Christian service is done by volunteers, it is certainly appropriate for pastors and others who labor extensively for the Lord to be compensated financially, and to be compensated generously when possible. Consider these statements by Jesus and Paul:

- *"...the laborer is worthy of his wages"* (Luke 10:7).

- *"...the Lord ordered that those who preach the Good News should be supported by those who benefit from it"* (1 Corinthians 9:14, NLT).

- *"Elders who do their work well should be respected and paid well, especially those who work hard at both preaching and teaching. For the Scripture says, 'You must not muzzle an ox to keep it from eating as it treads out the grain.' And in another place, 'Those who work deserve their pay!'"* (1 Timothy 5:17-18, NLT).

Observers have long noted that churches that take good care of their ministers, tend to thrive and do very well, while those that are "chintzy" and tight toward their ministers tend to not do so well.

On occasion, Paul voluntarily refrained from receiving financial compensation from certain churches. Sometimes this was probably just a logistical matter: the church was in its infancy and unable to offer much support. At other times, Paul was demonstrating the purity of his motives, so he would not be accused of ministering simply for the money. Paul received missionary support on some occasions (see Philippians 4:15-18), while on others, he was what we would call a "bi-vocational" minister. In at least three cities that Paul ministered in, he functioned bi-vocationally:

- Corinth - *"...because he [Paul] was of the same trade, he stayed with them [Aquila and Priscilla] and worked; for by occupation they were tentmakers"* (Acts 18:3).

- Ephesus - *"I have coveted no one's silver or gold or apparel. Yes, you yourselves know that these hands have provided for my necessities, and for those who were with me. I have shown you in every way, by laboring like this, that you must support the weak. And remember the words of the Lord Jesus, that He said, 'It is more blessed to give than to receive'"* (Acts 20:33-35).

- Thessalonica - *"We never accepted food from anyone without paying for it. We worked hard day and night so we would not be a burden to any of you. We certainly had the right to ask you to feed us, but we wanted to give you an example to follow"* (1 Thessalonians 3:8-9, NLT).

It is great when the work of pastors can be fully supported by the church. Logistically, pastors are able to accomplish much more in the Lord's work when they are able to completely focus on their ministry. However, we should never think less of the important contributions of those who serve bi-vocationally. I appreciate that Rick Warren wrote the following in The Purpose Driven Church: "I dedicate this book to the bi-vocational pastors around the world: shepherds who faithfully and lovingly serve in churches that aren't large enough to provide a full-time salary. You are the true heroes of faith in my view."[28]

As appropriate as it is for ministers to be compensated well for their work, there are times and occasions when conscientious spiritual leaders will refuse certain types of monies, based on moral or ethical grounds. For example:

- Abram (Abraham) said "no" to the King of Sodom. *"I will take nothing, from a thread to a sandal strap, and that I will not take anything that is yours, lest you should say, 'I have made Abram rich'"* (Genesis 14:23).

- An unnamed prophet refused money from King Jereboam, lest it appear that a healing was paid for (1 Kings 13:6-10).

- Elisha also refused silver, gold, and clothing from Naaman lest it appear that a healing was paid for. When, Gehazi, Elisha's servant, went behind Elisha's back to obtain these assets, he was exposed and leprosy came upon him (2 Kings 6:15-27).

---

[28] Warren, Rick, *The Purpose Driven Church*, (Grand Rapids: Zondervan Publishing, 1995), Dedication Page.

- Peter refused to accept money from Simon the Sorcerer, as payment for a spiritual gift (Acts 8:18-23).

- As mentioned previously, Paul sometimes refused compensation that he technically had a right to receive. He told the Corinthians, *"...when I was with you and didn't have enough to live on, I did not become a financial burden to anyone. For the brothers who came from Macedonia brought me all that I needed. I have never been a burden to you, and I never will be ...no one in all of Greece will ever stop me from boasting about this ...I will continue doing what I have always done. This will undercut those who are looking for an opportunity to boast that their work is just like ours"* (2 Corinthians 11:9-10, 12, also see 1 Corinthians 9:11-18).

Why would these men of God, in these unique situations, refuse money? Why would spiritual leaders today, in certain situations, refuse money?

- Sometimes it's a matter of principle

- Sometimes it would give the wrong impression

- Sometimes it's not in the best interests of the giver

Cicero, a Roman statesman who died a few decades before the birth of Christ, said, "But the chief thing in all public administration and public service is to avoid even the slightest suspicion of self-seeking." What a phenomenal insight. How important it is for leaders today not to engage in any practice that appears to be self-serving.

There are right ways, as well as wrong ways, to prosper. Proverbs 28:20 says, "A faithful man will abound with blessings, but he who hastens to be rich will not go unpunished." Likewise, Proverbs 10:22 tells us, "The blessing of the LORD makes one rich, and He adds no sorrow with it."

Spiritual leaders need to be aware of the pitfalls and entanglements, that can occur when they inappropriately use their influence to promote certain financial, business, or investment endeavors. Believers should not have to wonder whether a spiritual leader's interest in them is pastoral in nature, or if the spiritual leader is simply looking to capitalize on them as potential source of revenue. As a general rule, it's good to keep church issues and personal business/investment issues completely separate.

Occasionally, pastors are approached by people who want them to use their spiritual influence in order to recruit others to participate in a business deal or some kind of investment opportunity. In today's turbulent economy, even legitimate investments can go bad. If believers lose money because a spiritual leader whom they trusted encouraged them to make a particular investment, then that important relationship can be seriously strained. If people get offended because they lost money in a business deal that was promoted by the church or one of its leaders, then they are also likely to leave the church, or at least lose confidence in that leader.

Avoiding the Sting of Christian Con-Men

Jim Guinn is a CPA with decades of experience in helping churches and ministries with their accounting needs. Jim writes:

> In the past few years, unscrupulous promoters claiming to be Christians have taken literally millions of dollars from fellow Christians for illegitimate oil deals, gold mine schemes, multilevel marketing pyramid schemes and other get-rich-quick schemes. What a tragedy for ministers and church members, who have worked hard all their lives to provide for their retirement or for their children's education, to be conned out of their savings. If you are approached by an investment promoter, consider the following:

- If the investment sounds too good to be true, it is.

- If this single investment is supposed to make you rich, it is maybe a get-rich-quick scheme and probably not a sound investment.

- If the person promoting the investment requires cash before furnishing all the details of the investment to you, consider this a red flag. Never make even a down payment without fully understanding the investment's potential and risks.

- If the promoter does not provide financial statements showing the results of similar ventures, and financial statements showing his and/or his company's financial stability, do not invest.

- If the promoter discourages you from talking to your financial adviser, CPA or attorney because of the secretive nature of the investment, be suspicious. This is usually an indication the investment is not sound.

- If the promoter tells you the investment will make you rich, enabling you to give money to churches and ministries for spreading the Gospel and winning the world for God, do not invest. In a sense, he is asking you to bribe God to bless the investment.

- If the promoter does not provide you with verifiable references from previous investors, do not invest.

- When the promised rate of return in relationship to the amount of investment is unreasonably high, consider it a warning signal. This type of investment is almost always too good to be true.

- If the product or marketing plan to be financed by your investment is so complicated that you cannot completely understand how your money will be used, or how you will receive the return promised, do not get involved in the investment.

- When the promoter tries to rush you to invest because the investment opportunity is limited and going fast, do not invest. Always take the time necessary to check out the opportunity.

- Many promoters employ techniques designed to use your beliefs to their advantage.

Beware when:

- The promoter quotes Bible verses as support for the investment.

- The promoter's lapel is covered with pins from religious organizations, implying that he supports the same organizations you do.

- The promoter touts his relationship to various Christian organizations, such as his position on the board of a ministry (especially one that teaches a prosperity doctrine), to induce you to make the investment.

- The promoter mentions his strong membership status in a church, as an inducement to encourage you to invest (e.g., "I am a member of the same kind of church you are and since we are Christian brothers you should help me and help yourself by investing with me").

- The promoter informs you that you are one of the "select few" being offered this investment opportunity. If the promoter is legitimate, he will offer the investment to any qualified investor.

Spiritual considerations are not inappropriate when making investment decisions. We believe in asking for God's help. However, it is not right for Christians to be deceived by promoters, who clothe bad investments in "religious" garments. It is good for a person to support a ministry, and there is nothing wrong with wearing lapel pins. It is good that a person is a strong member of a church, and commendable that a person shares money that he has made from an investment with the church to further the Gospel. But your decision to make an investment based only on these criteria, instead of the economic criteria, can be an expensive, even bankrupting mistake. Most wealth comes from hard work.

Remember, a farmer cannot harvest a crop unless he has labored to plant the grain. Do not expect more than an honest return for an honest investment dollar. If a potential investment sounds too good to be true and is being promoted primarily with noneconomic considerations, get away from the promoter as quickly as possible. Be content with investments providing a legitimate and reasonable rate of return. Safe investments seldom offer exorbitant rates of return."[29]

No doubt, some well-meaning Christians - even leaders - have been duped into innocently promoting something that they truly thought would be helpful. Never allow someone's alleged Christianity to lull you into a sense of carelessness, causing you to neglect sound business principles and practices. Be on guard against people using the church and their relationship with the pastor to secure investments from people or to promote their business.

It is imperative that spiritual leaders are wise, that they keep their hearts free from covetousness and from practices that are self-serving. In

---

[29] Guinn, James, *Religious Organizations: IRS and Accounting Issues,* (Dallas: Guinn, Smith, and Company, 1998).

worst-case scenarios where a leader is exploiting the people, the rebuke given by God through Ezekiel can still apply today. "Son of man, prophesy against the shepherds, the leaders of Israel. Give them this message from the Sovereign LORD: What sorrow awaits you shepherds who feed yourselves instead of your flocks. Shouldn't shepherds feed their sheep? You drink the milk, wear the wool, and butcher the best animals, but you let your flocks starve" (Ezekiel 34:2-3, NLT).

Questions for Reflection and Discussion

1. It was noted that, "...churches who take good care of their ministers tend to thrive and do very well." Can you think of reasons why this would be so?

_____

_____

_____

_____

_____

_____

2. Proverbs 10:2 says, "The blessing of the LORD makes one rich, and He adds no sorrow with it." Have you ever seen a situation, in which a person received money in a way that actually hurt him or set him back in the long-run? _____

_____

_____

_____

_____

_____

_____

3. What can potentially happen if you are a spiritual leader and you promote an investment "opportunity" that goes bad? What can that do to relationships?_____

_____

_____

_____

_____

_____

_____

4. Think back through the warnings given by Jim Guinn regarding questionable investment and business dealings. Can you recall some of them?

_____

_____

_____

_____

_____

_____

_____

5. What is the main insight that you have gained from this chapter?_____

_____

_____

_____

_____

_____

_____

_____

Chapter Fourteen

PRACTICAL CONSIDERATIONS IN FINANCIAL WISDOM AND INTEGRITY

"We deem it a sacred responsibility and genuine opportunity to be faithful stewards of all that God has entrusted to us: our time, our talents, and our financial resources. We view all of life as a sacred trust to be used wisely."

- Moravian Covenant for Christian Living

Key Thought: *Spiritual leaders are conscientious, responsible, and diligent in their handling of finances.*

At the time of this writing, our country has been experiencing a lengthy season of extreme financial difficulty. Home values have plummeted and unemployment has remained high. In the past few years, an unprecedented number of people have filed for bankruptcy and have lost their homes due to foreclosures. As a result of this economic downturn, many churches and ministries, as well as Christians and spiritual leaders, have been adversely affected.

We are living in a day when leaders must not only have great faith to trust and believe God, but they must also have great wisdom to handle money wisely. Nothing in this chapter is intended to reflect negatively or bring condemnation to individuals or churches that have suffered financial setbacks. However, it is still extremely important for leaders and believers to operate in the highest levels of ethics and wisdom concerning financial matters.

Whether you are reading this in a financially challenging time or a period of great abundance, you have a predecessor in ministry who can relate to your situation. Paul said, "I know how to be abased, and I know how to abound. Everywhere and in all things I have learned both to be full and to be hungry, both to abound and to suffer need. I can do all things through Christ who strengthens me" (Philippians 4:12-13). The NLT renders part of verse 12, "I know how to live on almost nothing or with everything."

Accountability

Paul was very diligent to protect himself from the accusations of impropriety by having solid accountability in regard to his handling of finances. Paul spoke about an offering that he had received in Greece for believers in Jerusalem when he said, "We want to avoid any criticism of the way we administer this liberal gift. For we are taking pains to do what is right, not only in the eyes of the Lord but also in the eyes of men" (2 Corinthians 8:20-21, NIV).

To facilitate his desire for accountability, Paul encouraged each church to have a representative accompany him and help in the distribution of these funds. Paul could have taken the money all by himself to Jerusalem, and I believe he would have been completely honest in his dealings. However, to do so could have opened him up to criticism and placed him in a vulnerable position.

Wise Counsel

Proverbs 11:14 tells us, "Where there is no counsel, the people fall; but in the multitude of counselors there is safety." In a day of complex laws, it is beneficial for pastors, churches, and ministries to seek advice and guidance from various professionals, such as CPAs, attorneys, bankers, business advisors, insurance agents, etc. Some of this counsel will cost money, but it could be a lot more expensive to not have proper guidance. Churches and ministries should allocate adequate finances in order to receive such counsel and to procure professional services as needed. Proper procedures and systems should be established and followed. Likewise, sound business principles should also be implemented and all relevant laws observed.

It's always good to make sure that you are receiving sound counsel from reputable sources. Someone once said, "The two quickest ways to disaster, are to take nobody's advice, and to take everybody's advice." Sophocles said, "No enemy is worse than bad advice."

Responsibly Meeting Obligations

This may seem elementary, but paying our bills and our taxes is a part of operating in integrity. We should be diligent and prompt in these matters. When asked about paying taxes, Jesus said, "Render therefore to Caesar the things that are Caesar's, and to God the things that are God's" (Matthew 22:21).

Paul reiterated this when he said, "...you must live responsibly—not just to avoid punishment but also because it's the right way to live. That's also why you pay taxes—so that an orderly way of life can be maintained. Fulfill your obligations as a citizen. Pay your taxes, pay your bills, respect your leaders" (Romans 13:5-7, MSG).

In the next verse Paul says, "Owe no one anything except to love one another..." (Romans 13:8). Some have interpreted this to mean that a Christian should never, under any circumstance, borrow money. However, I believe that other versions shed additional and helpful light on the meaning of this verse.

The NIV reads, "Let no debt remain outstanding, except the continuing debt to love one another..." GOD'S WORD translation renders the same verse, "Pay your debts as they come due. However, one debt you can never finish paying is the debt of love that you owe each other..."

Understood this way, we receive the impression that we should simply pay our bills on time. However, there is obviously great wisdom in getting debt-free and living debt-free. Proverbs 22:7 says, "the borrower is servant to the lender," and this is especially true when debt has become overwhelming and unmanageable. Someone once said, "When your outgo exceeds your income, your upkeep becomes your downfall."

Irresponsible spending and credit card debt has become a huge problem in our nation. Credit can be a good tool, but if not properly managed, it can become a source of great bondage. In my travels, a credit card is a necessity for renting cars, paying for hotel rooms, etc. However, Lisa and I have made it a practice over the years not to put more on our credit card than we are prepared to pay off at the end of the month. This has served us very well and has also saved us a significant amount of money on interest.

Easy credit and an image-conscious society have contributed to many people becoming over-extended financially. Some have been obsessed with wanting to appear prosperous, so they have purchased homes, cars, clothes, jewelry, etc. that were simply beyond their means.

George Washington Carver, who died in 1943, said, "We have become ninety-nine percent money mad. The method of living at home modestly and within our income, laying a little by systematically for the proverbial rainy day which is due to come, can almost be listed among the lost arts."

Calvin Coolidge, President of the United States from 1923-1929, stated, "There is no dignity quite so impressive and no independence quite so important as living within your means."

A good rule of thumb for individuals who are seeking to manage their money wisely, is to give 10% to God, put 10% in savings, and live within your means on the other 80%.

Entanglements to Avoid

Some individuals have endeavored to help others by co-signing on a loan with them. While this sounds virtuous, it can lead to serious problems. First of all, if the person you co-sign for cannot pay their bill, you are obligated to pay it. Second, if they do not pay their bill and you have to, they are probably going to be uncomfortable being around you in the future and if you are a pastor or spiritual leader, that probably means that they will avoid church (this applies when you make a loan to someone as well). If this reasoning isn't sufficient to keep you from co-signing, then consider the following Scriptures:

> *My child, if you have put up security for a friend's debt or agreed to guarantee the debt of a stranger—if you have trapped yourself by your agreement and are caught by what you said—follow my advice and save yourself, for you have placed yourself at your friend's mercy. Now swallow your pride; go and beg to have your name erased. Don't put it off; do it now! Don't rest until you do. Save yourself like a gazelle escaping from a hunter, like a bird fleeing from a net.*

> Proverbs 6:1-5 (NLT)

There's danger in putting up security for a stranger's debt; it's safer not to guarantee another person's debt.

Proverbs 11:15 (NLT)

It's poor judgment to guarantee another person's debt or put up security for a friend.

Proverbs 17:18 (NLT)

Don't agree to guarantee another person's debt or put up security for someone else. If you can't pay it, even your bed will be snatched from under you.

Proverbs 22:26-27 (NLT)

Receiving Tithes and Offerings

- Teach boldly and confidently about stewardship, tithes, offerings, generosity, etc. Don't be ashamed, apologetic, or backward in teaching about money and related topics; it is part of the whole counsel of God that we are responsible to teach.

- Be honest and straightforward about special projects and needs of the church and make sure that designated offerings go to the project(s) for which they were received.

- Don't pressure people into giving through guilt, shame, condemnation, threats, etc.

- Don't "hype" or manipulate people into impulsive-type giving that they will later regret and probably be resentful about. A person is supposed to give "as he purposes in his heart" (2 Corinthians 9:7), not in a state of frenzied emotionalism.

- Don't make unfounded, unrealistic promises to people. Avoid anything that could be construed as spiritual manipulation.

- Avoid gimmicks.

Pastor – Guest Minister Relations

In an article entitled, "Etiquette for Pastors: How to Honor Guest Ministers in Your Church," Pastor Michael Cameneti wrote: "We believe that any minister who sows the Word into our congregation is someone God wants to bless, so we strive to bless that guest minister 'above and beyond.' I consistently seek to impart to our congregation the heart to give and be a blessing by ministering on finances based on First Timothy 5:18. Then I encourage everyone in our church family to participate by giving in guest-minister offerings. Additionally, we believe it's always better to sow more into an offering than the initial amount received, so we always add to the guests' offerings just to bless them. We feel strongly in our hearts that we cannot out-give God, and that He will supply all our needs as we sow into the lives of others." [30]

Likewise, guest ministers should be highly respectful of the local church and its pastor as well. Over the years, I've heard pastors share about negative experiences with guest ministers who appeared to be more interested in what they could get out of the church financially, than what they could invest into the church spiritually.

I recently spoke at a church and received written guidelines ahead of time. I thought that these guidelines were very good. It was obvious from the points that were presented in these guidelines, that the pastor felt that his people had been "fleeced" before. As a good pastor, he was just doing

---

[30]Cameneti, Michael, "Etiquette for Pastors: How to Honor Guest Ministers in Your Church," IMPART NOW.com. January-February 2009.

his best to make sure that type of thing did not happen again. Some of his guidelines included:

- Depending on the type of service, an honorarium will be given to the guest minister, or the pastor will receive an offering for the guest minister at the conclusion of the service. Guest ministers are not allowed to receive their own offering.

- Only church offering envelopes will be used if an offering is received.

- Only three minutes of pulpit time is permitted to promote products unless the pastor gives prior consent.

- Church members are not allowed to be put on a guest minister's mailing list without their clear, personal consent.

- The church will provide, per table, two experienced church volunteers to assist with setting up and selling any of the guest minister's materials and products. This is done because we are very sensitive regarding interaction with people from our community.

- Checks for products will be made payable to the church. All monies from the sales of products will be mailed out with the honorarium within 3-5 business days.

I'm not presenting these thoughts as absolute "musts," but there is a great need for pastors and guest ministers to work with mutual respect toward one another. The ideal will be achieved when each party seeks to bless the other party greatly.

Questions for Reflection and Discussion

1. What simple step did Paul take to avoid criticism in the way he handled ministry funds?_____

_____

_____

_____

_____

_____

2. Is there scriptural support for paying one's taxes? What verses come to mind?_____

_____

_____

_____

_____

_____

_____

3. What does the Bible say about co-signing (becoming responsible for another person's debts should they be unwilling or unable to pay)?

_____

_____

_____

_____

_____

_____

_____

4. What is the main insight that you have gained from this chapter?

_____

_____

_____

_____

_____

_____

_____

_____

_____

Chapter Fifteen

THE LEADER'S ATTITUDE TOWARD MONEY-

ARE INDULGENCES MAKING A COMEBACK?

People who long to be rich fall into temptation and are trapped by many foolish and harmful desires that plunge them into ruin and destruction. For the love of money is the root of all kinds of evil. And some people, craving money, have wandered from the true faith and pierced themselves with many sorrows. But you, Timothy, are a man of God; so run from all these evil things. Pursue righteousness and a godly life, along with faith, love, perseverance, and gentleness.

- 1 Timothy 6:9-11 (NLT)

Key Thought: *Exploiting people for money is a long-standing evil. Leaders must avoid it, and believers must be wise to not be taken advantage of.*

One of my favorite movies chronicles Martin Luther's ministry, leading up to, and through the Protestant Reformation.[31] In the movie, Luther's distress over the unscriptural practice of indulgences is clearly seen. Indulgences, "...authorized by papal author-

---

[31] Till, Eric, *Luther* (Los Angeles, CA: RS Entertainment, 2003).

ity in 1411, had begun in the eleventh century with the teaching that pious service, say, in the Crusades would reduce one's stay in purgatory. In the fifteenth century, guarantees of shorter stays in purgatory in exchange for monies became a regular component of fundraising techniques for the papacy." [32]

The idea of "buying" blessings or spiritual favors did not begin, though, in the Middle Ages. In Acts 8, an individual known as Simon the Sorcerer (who had believed the gospel and had been baptized) made Peter an offer that was sternly and harshly rejected.

> *When Simon saw that the Spirit was given when the apostles laid their hands on people, he offered them money to buy this power. "Let me have this power, too," he exclaimed, "so that when I lay my hands on people, they will receive the Holy Spirit!" But Peter replied, "May your money be destroyed with you for thinking God's gift can be bought! You can have no part in this, for your heart is not right with God. Repent of your wickedness and pray to the Lord. Perhaps he will forgive your evil thoughts, for I can see that you are full of bitter jealousy and are held captive by sin."*

Acts 8:18-23 (NLT)

The New Testament in Modern English renders verse 20, "To hell with you and your money!" Translator J.B. Phillips says that this is exactly what the Greek means. The Message Version and the Good News Translation also provide similar renderings of that verse. Even today, the term "Simony" refers not only to the practice of purchasing ecclesiastical offices, but also is used broadly to denote any kind of trafficking in sacred things.

---

[32]Bingham, Jeffrey, *Pocket History of the Church*, (Downers Grove: IVP Academic, 2002) 113.

More Abuses

Going back further in biblical history, we see other distortions, corruptions, and abuses regarding money and spiritual things. In 1 Samuel 2:12-17, we see that the sons of Eli (the high priest in those days) were very corrupt, abused the sacrificial system, and exploited the people of God. Verse 17 (GW) says, *"This sin of Eli's sons was a serious matter to the LORD because these men were treating the offerings made to the LORD with contempt."* Instead of treating the offerings of the people as holy, sacred gifts being presented unto the Lord, Eli's sons contemptuously and forcefully intimidated those who were endeavoring to obey God in order to indulge their own greed.

Jesus himself confronted another corrupt system that fleeced and mistreated worshippers. The story of Jesus driving the money-changers out of the temple is well-known, but many have not noticed what happened after the greed, covetousness, and unethical practices were eradicated.

> *Then Jesus went into the temple of God and drove out all those who bought and sold in the temple, and overturned the tables of the money changers and the seats of those who sold doves. And He said to them, "It is written, "My house shall be called a house of prayer,' but you have made it a 'den of thieves.' Then the blind and the lame came to Him in the temple, and He healed them.*
>
> Matthew 21:12-14

Did you notice that? When man's corruption was removed, the glory of God was manifested. There is great shame in vulnerable people being taken advantage of, but how grievous it is that people miss seeing the glory of God because the manipulative practices of man are obscuring the vision of sincere-hearted worshippers.

The Apostle Paul was painfully aware of "so-called" ministers whose motives and methods were driven by greed. He made it a point to differentiate himself from those who were manipulative, and whose shady and unscrupulous practices brought reproach to the things of God. The same man who wrote about "the grace of giving" had to address the "dis-grace" of wolves in sheep's clothing who preyed upon gullible, impressionable, and naïve saints.

> For we are not, like so many, [like hucksters making a trade of] peddling God's Word [shortchanging and adulterating the divine message]; but like [men] of sincerity and the purest motive, as [commissioned and sent] by God, we speak [His message] in Christ (the Messiah), in the [very] sight and presence of God.
>
> 2 Corinthians 2:17 (AMP)

Later, Paul said to them: "I do not seek yours, but you" (2 Corinthians 12:14). To the Thessalonians, Paul said, "God is our witness that we were not pretending to be your friends just to get your money" (2 Thessalonians 2:5, NLT). Paul went to great lengths to avoid any self-serving actions, even to the point of refusing appropriate remuneration so no one could accuse him of being in ministry just for the money (1 Corinthians 9:1-18).

The Apostle Peter spoke of false teachers who would cause the way of truth to be blasphemed (2 Peter 2:2), and in the next verse said, "By covetousness they will exploit you with deceptive words." In other translations, 2 Peter 2:3 is rendered:

- In their greed they will make up clever lies to get hold of your money. (NLT)

- And in their covetousness (lust, greed), they will exploit you with false (cunning) arguments. (AMP)

- And through covetousness, shall they with feigned words, make merchandise of you. (KJV)

- They will say anything that sounds good to exploit you. (MSG)

It is important to understand that even the shadiest and most disreputable financial appeals are going to contain some degree of truth. You may even hear token "disclaimers" that seem to add legitimacy to their message. For example, they might say, "Now I'm not trying to tell you that you can buy a miracle..." or, "This really isn't about your money; it's about your faith." But in the final analysis, the overall impression that the potential donor receives, is that there is some type of special miracle or blessing that is only going to be received by giving money in that particular offering.

Further, impulsive giving is going to be strongly promoted ("Act now, go to your phone right now, give now while the anointing is strong, don't let this miracle moment pass you by, don't let the devil talk you out of this blessing, etc."). Recently, one minister proclaimed that there was a two-minute time window, during which contributors could give a $1,000 offering and receive special miraculous results. Of course, people had to act immediately to receive the special "blessing" that was connected only with this offering.

A few years ago, I heard a minister on television extolling the virtues of the number "seven" as it is used throughout the Bible. He concluded that because the year was 2007, his viewers were being instructed by God to give a certain monetary amount (relative to the number 7), in order to receive their "miracle breakthrough." It was not recommended though, that anyone send in a $7 offering (which would be logical, if there really was even the remotest connection to the calendar year, relative to how much a believer was supposed to give). Somehow, $77, $777, and $7,777 were the suggested amounts.

Of course, great blessings were promised to those who gave one of the allegedly inspired amounts. This man's line of thought made me wonder if no financial offerings should be given in the year 2010, since it ends in zero - but I'm pretty sure that he would have a different kind of revelation for that year.

As I listened to this very deceptive presentation, I wondered if Martin Luther was questioning if what he had preached against the selling of indulgences (essentially, the selling of forgiveness) was in vain. At one time, individuals were told that by giving a special offering to the church, they could reduce the time of their stay in purgatory. They also had the option of helping to provide an early release for departed loved ones who were still in purgatory. John Tetzel was the leading seller of indulgences, and he often said, "As soon as a coin in the coffer rings, the soul from purgatory springs."

Luther, incensed over this spiritually corrupt and manipulative form of extortion, posted his Ninety-five Theses (these were points for debate), on the north door of the Castle Church in Wittenberg (the doors there were often used as a bulletin board for notices). While other issues were addressed, many of his ninety-five points dealt specifically with the "selling of indulgences." Here are a few samples of what Luther presented:

- *"...those who preach indulgences are in error when they say that a man is absolved and saved from every penalty by the pope's indulgences."*

- *"There is no divine authority for preaching that the soul flies out of the purgatory immediately the money clinks in the bottom of the chest."*

- *"The indulgences, which the merchants extol as the greatest of favors, are seen to be, in fact, a favorite means for money-getting."*

- *"It is blasphemy to say that the insignia of the cross with the papal arms are of equal value to the cross on which Christ died."*

Today, people may not be trying to reduce their time in purgatory; however, it is still a serious matter if people are led to believe that every blessing, miracle, or breakthrough is somehow connected to giving money. As I watched this preacher on television, I thought to myself, *I've heard of encouragement, edification, and exhortation, but this is nothing more than extraction — extracting money out of the peoples' wallets!* Further, I wondered why these presentations on television always ended with the persuasive phrase, "Go to your phone," and never, "Go to your church."

One minister said, "You can receive information from anyone, but you can only receive revelation from a minister that you sow into." I thought to myself, *If that's the case, then none of us would be able to receive revelation from any of Paul's writings, because none of us have ever given financially to him.* There is a serious problem when the impression is conveyed that every blessing, every breakthrough, every miracle, and every answer to prayer is contingent upon a financial gift being given.

It is unfortunate when something so beautiful as God's "sharing grace" is missed because people have been repeatedly exposed to cheap substitutes. When people are pressured by manipulative gimmicks, hype, or other techniques to coerce them into giving, the true plan of God is frustrated.

In an article entitled, "Christian TV's All-Time Worst Fundraising Gimmicks," J. Lee Grady said, "Let's stop the hypnotism, the guilt manipulation and the high-pressure gimmicks. It's time to reclaim our lost credibility." He went on to say that some Christian networks, "...have shamelessly extorted money from viewers over the years using heavy-handed guilt manipulation, hypnotic control and bizarre Scripture-twisting." Grady concluded his remarks with, "Hopefully, emerging leaders in the religious broadcasting industry will restore our lost credibility by insisting on integrity, authenticity and good taste."[33]

---

[33]Grady, J. Lee, "Christian TV's All Time Worst Fundraising Gimmicks," *Charisma & Christian Life,* August, 2010.

How much damage has actually been produced by such manipulative tactics in the pulpit? Countless unbelievers have become jaded toward Christianity, hardened to the Gospel, and assume that preachers are simply "in it for the money." This alone is tragic. In addition, some sincere believers have become disappointed and disillusioned when promises of miracle prosperity did not materialize as expected. Many of these disheartened believers have become closed, reluctant, and hesitant to give anymore.

Understandably, many feel exploited, taken advantage of, and defrauded. They will not be quick to trust preachers again. Perhaps they mistakenly saw giving as a "get-rich-quick" opportunity. Some sink into a state of guilt and condemnation because they believe that their faith must have not been sufficient to bring in the expected harvest. Others become hardened and give up on giving entirely. All of these are lamentable and grievous outcomes that result when "dis-graceful" exploitation is substituted for the beautiful grace of giving that Paul taught (2 Corinthians 8:6-7).

A missionary friend once shared with me that in his country, young ministers watched American preachers on television and picked up on some of their "slick" techniques in taking offerings. The following guidelines are shared, not only to help ministers avoid some of these inappropriate methods, but also to help believers gain wisdom and discernment in order to protect themselves from being manipulated.

Red Flags Indicating a "Fleecing" is About to Take Place

• It should be a red flag when the impression is given that as a result of giving in a specific offering, you will receive some special kind of blessing, miracle, or breakthrough that you would not otherwise be entitled to if you were simply giving to your church or supporting some other ministry. Frequently used incentives include things like: all your debts will be supernaturally paid off, you will receive a needed healing, or your children or spouse will get saved... all because you gave money. Again, watch out for the "token disclaimer." You will probably be told, "Now you can't buy a miracle, this is a matter of faith!" Nevertheless, the specifically prescribed way you release your faith is by giving money in this particular offering. Decades ago, Gordon Lindsay wrote, "Perhaps the most serious scheme to raise money is one promoted by a certain religious adventurer who promises the people that God has given him the gift to make them wealthy, if only they will give him a good offering. Such assertions approach to the crime of blasphemy."[34]

- It should be a red flag when "specially anointed" oil or prayer cloths are used in conjunction with offerings. While cloths (Acts 19:11-12) and anointing with oil (James 5:14-15) are definitely mentioned positively in the New Testament, caution must be exercised to ensure that these things don't become gimmicks to initiate an appeal for funds. In some situations, these are initially offered for free by certain ministries, but strong financial appeals soon follow. Likewise, some have offered "prophecies" for a donation, and in some cases, the first "prophecy" is just a teaser. Guess what you have to do to get the more detailed "prophecy" that will really release God's blessings in your life? That's right: send more money. No one is so audacious as to say outright that they are selling the blessings of God, but when all the veneer and spiritual lingo is removed, that is essentially what's happening.

---

[34]Lindsay, Gordon, *God's 20th Century Barnabas*, (Dallas: Christ for the Nations, Reprint 1982), 276.

- It should be a red flag when any type of ministry diminishes your sense of priesthood. Instead of you having your own relationship with God in which you can exercise faith, use wisdom, and be led by the Spirit yourself, you are dependent on the minister with the "special prosperity anointing" to direct you into receiving your blessing. Legitimate ministry supports and reinforces your sense of priesthood before God; it doesn't create an unhealthy dependency on some "super minister" who, in essence, becomes your link to God and God's blessings. First Timothy 2:5 says, "...there is one God and one Mediator between God and men, the Man Christ Jesus." Legitimate ministry cultivates your dependency on God, His Word, and your ability to follow the leading of the Holy Spirit. Unhealthy ministry promotes a dependency on some specially anointed minister, who alone can facilitate God's blessings coming to you (especially when your faith is "activated" and "released" by the financial seed you sow into "God's servant"). Intimidation may even be used, projecting to the listener that he is being disobedient if he does not participate or is being "religious" if he questions the supposedly infallible word of God's anointed servant.

- It should be a red flag when marvelous testimonies are offered from individuals who experienced extraordinary miracles as a result of giving to a particular ministry. The implication is that if you give, then you will also experience the same kind of results. I've noticed on TV commercials for weight loss products that a testimony is often given in which a person shares their story of drastic weight loss via that particular diet plan. At the bottom of the television screen in small letters is typically the phrase, "Results Not Typical." Perhaps that is a legal requirement for secular advertising, but it would be refreshing to hear a minister acknowledge that most people who give are not going to find an unexpected $75,000 check in the mail or get their house miraculously paid off because they gave in that one "special" offering. It is also unfortunate that some ministries have resorted to brochures and "infomercials" that feature pictures of mansions, swimming pools, luxury sports cars, diamond jewelry, gold bars, and huge stacks of cash. Such tasteless promotions (in the name of the Lord) shamelessly appeal to greed and remind me of Paul's warning to Timothy regarding, "...men who are corrupted in mind and bereft of the truth, who imagine that godliness or righteousness is a source of profit [a moneymaking business, a means of livelihood]. From such withdraw" (1 Timothy 6:5, Amplified).

- It should be a red flag when the minister suggests a donation amount based on a particular Bible verse or through the use of numerology. For example, after preaching on Isaiah 55:11, a minister suggests that if the listener needs a miracle, he should give an offering of $55.11. It's interesting that ministers who use this technique are far more likely to preach from Psalm 107:20 than they are from Psalm 1:1. After all, an offering of $107.20 is much better than an offering of $1.01. Offerings based on some numerological interpretation of the Bible are almost always the result of human manipulation, not divine inspiration. I would have no problem if, for instance, on a church's 50th Anniversary, the leadership of the church suggested that everyone prayerfully consider giving an extra $5, $50, or $500 to do what they can toward some special project. However this should only be a suggestion. It becomes problematic when the "highly anointed minister" plays "the Lord told me" card, and authoritatively proclaims that everyone who gives $500 or

$5,000 is going to receive some type of blessing that can only be accessed by giving this particular divinely decreed amount. That's when it becomes manipulative and coercive. Always beware of anyone who endeavors to prophesy money out of your pocket - and into theirs!

•   It should be a red flag when dates of certain Jewish feasts or other Old Testament events are used to promote special offerings in the New Testament era. Since most of us are New Testament believers from non-Jewish backgrounds, these days are not to govern our walk with God (Galatians 4:9-11; Colossians 2:16-17). In writing to a congregation of mixed background (Jewish and Gentile), Paul indicated that there should be tolerance and respect when it comes to background issues and personal convictions (Romans 14:1-9), but there is no New Testament basis for proclaiming that God will especially bless "Old Testament-based" offerings in the Church age.

•   It should be a red flag when a message is peppered with not-so-subtle hints about how God has blessed people who have given to the minister or his ministry. Those types of hints (to borrow the terminology of fundraisers) are called "greasing the chute." In other words, it is psychologically conditioning the people to give. It should also be of concern when excessive time is spent by ministers talking about all the wealth and material blessings that they have received. Ministers are called to "preach the word" (2 Timothy 4:2), not to parade their possessions. Paul said that love, "...is not boastful or vainglorious, does not display itself haughtily" (1 Corinthians 13:4, AMP). Paul also said, "...our Message is not about ourselves; we're proclaiming Jesus Christ, the Master. All we are is messengers, errand runners from Jesus for you." (2 Corinthians 4:5, Message). God never ordained that ministers have a "rock star" or "celebrity" mentality; we are called to be servants. We are certainly not called to manipulate people for our own personal gain or benefit.

Blessings Without Money

We should be greatly blessed as we remember Isaiah 55:1-2: Ho! Everyone who thirsts, come to the waters; and you who have no money, come, buy and eat. Yes, come, buy wine and milk without money and without price. Why do you spend money for what is not bread, and your wages for what does not satisfy? Listen carefully to Me, and eat what is good, and let your soul delight itself in abundance.

As long as we hold to the understanding that God's greatest blessings are free gifts, then we can give from the right heart and the right motive, and we can avoid being pressured, manipulated, or taken advantage of by religious con-men!

Reclaiming God's Plan

We need to stay strongly committed to the word of God and remain positively focused. I am unashamedly in favor of tithing, giving, and biblical prosperity. If every believer in the Body of Christ would simply tithe to their local church (give 10% of their income) and give offerings as the Lord leads them, the work of God would be wonderfully supplied and progress in tremendous ways.

The Bible teaches us that there are blessings associated with giving, and that God "...has pleasure in the prosperity of His servant" (Psalm

35:27). Churches, missionaries, and ministries need finances to operate and to fulfill the Great Commission.

The Body of Christ needs to be deeply grateful for all of the credible pastors, missionaries, and other fine ministers (including many who are on television), who share the Gospel and the Word of God in a straightforward manner, with simplicity and sincerity. Thank God for those who are keeping the waters pure!

The Body of Christ must be strong, and see through the clutter and distractions of human imperfections as we walk out God's original purpose for our lives! The fact that some have operated in questionable or inappropriate methods should never keep us from believing His Word and doing the right thing.

God is still, "...able to make all grace (every favor and earthly blessing) come to you in abundance, so that you may always and under all circumstances and whatever the need be self-sufficient [possessing enough to require no aid or support and furnished in abundance for every good work and charitable donation]" (2 Corinthians 9:8, AMP). Let's freely yield ourselves to the grace of giving. We should not only receive from His generosity, but we should also live a life of generous giving.

Questions for Reflection and Discussion

1. Is exploiting people for money in the name of religion a new practice or an older one? How can believers today give biblically and generously without being taken advantage of?_____

_____

_____

_____

_____

_____

_____

_____

2. What was Peter's reaction when Simon tried to buy a spiritual gift or blessing?_____

_____

_____

_____

_____

_____

_____

_____

3. How many of the "red flags" concerning offerings do you remember? Have you seen any of those in practice before, and how did you feel about what you saw?_____

_____

_____

_____

_____

_____

_____

_____

_____

_____

4. What do you believe is God's way - the biblical way - of funding the work of the church and the spread of the Gospel?_____

_____

_____

_____

_____

_____

_____

_____

5. What is the main insight that you have gained from this chapter? _____

_____

_____

_____

_____

_____

_____

_____

_____

MINISTRY KILLERS YOU MUST CONQUER- THE GIRLS[35]

---

[35]Traditionally, most ministers, and especially pastors have been men. Therefore the term "The Girls" has been used as a phrase indicating a potential temptation for ministers. In reality, this chapter deals with any and every kind of moral and sexual problem, whether it is sexual misconduct with any person - male or female - or inappropriate conduct involving pornography.

Chapter Sixteen

MAINTAINING MORAL PURITY

"If a man can deceive his wife and children, break a vow he made to God in the presence of witnesses, and knowingly betray the trust of those who love him, what guarantee does his organization have that he will be honest in his dealings with them? People who prove themselves deceitful in one area of life are equally capable of being deceitful in other areas." [36]

- Henry and Richard Blackaby

Key Thought: *Spiritual leaders recognize that their body is the temple of the Holy Spirit and they keep themselves pure, not only physically, but in every dimension of their being.*

How much damage has been done to the Body of Christ due to immorality among its leaders?

- The Roman Catholic Church has been plagued by a seemingly endless parade of sexual abuse allegations against its priests.

- Empires of high profile televangelists and ministers have collapsed in the midst of salacious allegations of immorality.

[36]Blackaby, Henry and Richard, *Spiritual Leadership*, (Nashville, TN: B & H Publishing Group, 2001), 105.

- In communities throughout the country, local churches have been rocked when a youth minister was inappropriately involved with a teenager, a child was molested by a worker, or a pastor was found guilty of immorality involving a church or staff member.

Not only do such incidents harden unbelievers toward the gospel and disillusion young believers, but they are also highly distracting and demoralizing to churches as they seek to fulfill their mission. Left in the wake of immorality is a collection of devastated lives: betrayed spouses, bewildered children, devastated victims, innocent believers whose trust has been shattered, and an understandably jaded public.

Modern technology has contributed to a whole new array of moral issues such as Internet pornography, flirtatious texting, and social media liaisons. While some try to minimize the seriousness of some of these activities, common sense tells us that these activities are intrinsically problematic and can be a slippery slope that leads to increasingly toxic results while opening the door to even more serious troubles.

Sexual misconduct allegations against church leaders and employees have become increasingly common in the nation's courtrooms. Churches typically have insurance policies to protect themselves against charges of sexual misconduct and sexual harassment. Settlements can be in the hundreds of thousands of dollars - sometimes even in the millions - when it involves the sexual misconduct of clergy.

Nothing New

Problems of morality relating to ministry have been around for a long time. In the Old Testament, the sons of the High Priest abused their office and lived self-indulgently. First Samuel 2:12-13 (NLT) says that Eli's sons, "...were scoundrels who had no respect for the LORD or for their duties as priests..." Verse 22 says, "Eli was very old, but he was aware of what his sons were doing to the people of Israel. He knew, for instance, that his sons were seducing the young women who assisted at the entrance of the Tabernacle." Eli spoke to his sons, but did nothing beyond that, so their sinful behavior continued.

In today's society, Eli's sons would fit our modern description of predators. "...his sons were seducing the young women..." A predator is not someone who has merely yielded to temptation, sinned, and then truly repented. Rather, predators are those who deliberately and intentionally use (or I should say, abuse) their position, along with its incipient authority and influence, in order to seek out vulnerable individuals for the purpose of manipulating and using them to gratify their own needs.

Spiritual leaders need to understand that their example is extremely important. When some leaders have fallen morally, individuals, who respect their ministries, may be prone to think, "Well, if Rev. So-and-So couldn't resist temptation, then why should I even try?" Perhaps this is what prompted Geoffrey Chaucer (1342-1400), often considered the greatest English poet before Shakespeare, to write the following in regards to the need for high moral standards among pastors: "Going on foot, and in his hand a staff. This was the good example that he set: He practiced first what later he would teach. Out of the gospel he took that precept; And what's more, he would cite this saying too: 'If gold can rust, then what will iron do?' For if a priest be rotten, whom we trust, No wonder if a laymen comes to rust." [37]

Admonitions to Spiritual Leaders

Paul had some very specific guidance for his spiritual sons, Timothy and Titus, concerning their moral integrity and conduct.

---

[37]Chaucer, Geoffrey, *The Canterbury Tales*, (Oxford, England: Oxford University Press. 1985), 13.

Paul told Timothy, who was a young minister, to "Treat older women as you would your mother, and treat younger women with all purity as you would your own sisters" (1 Timothy 5:2, NLT).

I once received a call from an individual, and upon asking how things were going at the church he attended, he indicated that some people were upset with the pastor. The problem? The pastor often encouraged fellowship during a break in the service by saying, "Why don't you find five people and give them a hug." Then the pastor would routinely step off the platform and make a beeline to hug several of the pretty young ladies. People noticed that the pastor never went to the section where the older ladies or the men were sitting. Consequently, this leader's focus and partiality toward the younger, attractive ladies was causing his character and intentions to be called into question.

Paul also told Timothy, "Run from anything that stimulates youthful lusts. Instead, pursue righteous living, faithfulness, love, and peace. Enjoy the companionship of those who call on the Lord with pure hearts" (2 Timothy 2:22, NLT).

Many will focus on the first part of this verse (running away from youthful lusts), but overlook the positive directive: *"pursue righteous living, faithfulness, etc."* As important as biblical standards are, I feel sorry for any Christian who simply lives "to not do the don'ts." If we get focused on doing the "do's," then we will not be sitting around thinking about the "don'ts." Be immersed in becoming the godly, anointed, effective, productive and fruitful person that God has ordained you to be. Yes, run away from the wrong things, but don't forget to run toward the right things. Don't just think about what you are avoiding; get excited about the things of God that you are pursuing!

Titus, another of Paul's spiritual sons, also received a letter from Paul telling him how to conduct himself in pastoral ministry. In Titus 2:1-10, Paul admonished Titus how to minister to four specific groups of people: older men, older women, young men, and servants. It's fascinating to notice that Titus was not given instructions on what he was supposed to teach the younger women. Instead, Paul told Titus that the, "...older women must train the younger women to love their husbands and their children, to live wisely and be pure, to work in their homes, to do good, and to be submissive to their husbands. Then they will not bring shame on the word of God" (Titus 2:4-5).

Isn't it interesting that Paul would tell Titus how to minister to all of these groups of people, but then say, "Titus, when it comes to the younger women, let the older women minister to them." Was Paul, as a wise spiritual father, endeavoring to keep Titus out of situations where temptations would be increased?

In addition to the above statements, remember what Paul said about the qualifications of elders in 1 Timothy 3:2 (NLT): "So an elder must be a man whose life is above reproach. He must be faithful to his wife. He must exercise self-control, live wisely, and have a good reputation." The phrase, "faithful to his wife," means "one-woman-man." In other words, a spiritual leader is not only not supposed to have adulterous affairs, but he's also not supposed to be a flirt or a womanizer. He is not supposed to be the kind of person who is given to any kind of illicit relationship, and this includes inappropriate emotional attachments, inappropriate types of communication, and inappropriate physical or sexual relationships.

Guidelines for Believers Apply to Spiritual Leaders Also

It is important to remember that God doesn't have a set of guidelines for believers that are somehow irrelevant or non-applicable to leaders. If anything, God expects more out of His leaders, not less; He expects them to operate by higher standards, not by lower ones.

I remember hearing of one so-called minister who was obviously very deceived. He acknowledged that, generally speaking, God did not want people to commit adultery, but had made an exception for him. He said that God had revealed to him that because his ministry was so special and so anointed, God was allowing him to have a relationship on the side, because God knew that he could minister more effectively if his sexual needs were met. Such narcissistic pride brings great blindness. The fallacy of such presumption and arrogance will eventually be exposed. No, God doesn't have one set of rules for everyone else and a special set of exceptions for others. When it comes to moral standards, God's Word applies to everyone. Here are some of God's guidelines for all New Testament believers:

Run from sexual sin! No other sin so clearly affects the body as this one does. For sexual immorality is a sin against your own body. Don't you realize that your body is the temple of the Holy Spirit, who lives in you and was given to you by God? You do not belong to yourself, for God bought you with a high price. So you must honor God with your body.

1 Corinthians 6:18-20 (NLT)

When you follow the desires of your sinful nature, the results are very clear: sexual immorality, impurity, lustful pleasures...Those who belong to Christ Jesus have nailed the passions and desires of their sinful nature to his cross and crucified them there.

Galatians 5:19, 24 (NLT)

But among you there must not be even a hint of sexual immorality, or of any kind of impurity, or of greed, because these are improper for God's holy people. Nor should there be obscenity, foolish talk or coarse joking, which are out of place, but rather thanksgiving.

Ephesians 5:3-4 (NIV)

So put to death the sinful, earthly things lurking within you. Have nothing to do with sexual immorality, impurity, lust, and evil desires...

Colossians 3:5 (NLT)

God's will is for you to be holy, so stay away from all sexual sin. Then each of you will control his own body and live in holiness and honor—not in lustful passion like the pagans who do not know God and his ways. Never harm or cheat a Christian brother in this matter by violating his wife, for the Lord avenges all such sins, as we have solemnly warned you before. God has called us to live holy lives, not impure lives. Therefore, anyone who refuses to live by these rules is not disobeying human teaching but is rejecting God, who gives his Holy Spirit to you.

1 Thessalonians 4:3-8 (NLT)

Steps to Maintaining Moral Integrity in Your Life

- **Make a Quality Decision**

  Don't wait until you find yourself in a place of temptation to decide your course of action. Make your consecrations to God now and then live by them.

  Have a quality decision made ahead of time about maintaining moral purity throughout your life and ministry. If you have missed it in the past, receive the forgiveness and cleansing that God offers and determine now - with His help - to live the rest of your life in honor and integrity.

- **Maintain a solid relationship with God and your spouse.**

  Manage your spiritual health. Keep your relationship with God fresh and vibrant. Feed your spirit, not your carnality. Avoid spiritual, emotional, and physical burn-out. A fatigued person can be more susceptible to temptation.

A strong, thriving relationship with your spouse is vital. The relationship should be a growing one where love is kept fresh, where conflicts are resolved, and where resentment and anger are not allowed to fester. Openness, honesty, and mutual accountability are important. If your marriage relationship becomes strained, seek help. Men, if your wife warns you about someone that she feels has wrong intentions, take heed! Ladies, if your husband has a concern about the way another man is acting around you, pay attention!

- **Recognize your vulnerability.**

  A very likely candidate for moral failure is the person who deems himself invincible to temptation, who naively or proudly thinks: "That could never happen to me!" These two scriptural warnings come to mind:

  Therefore let him who thinks he stands take heed lest he fall.

  1 Corinthians 10:12

  Pride goes before destruction, And a haughty spirit before a fall.

  Proverbs 16:18

  As a spiritual leader, you are a "high value" target, and Satan would love to take you out of commission.

- **Remind yourself of the painful consequences of immorality.**

  Adultery is a brainless act, soul-destroying, self-destructive; Expect a bloody nose, a black eye, and a reputation ruined for good.

  Proverbs 6:32-33 (MSG)

The following is adapted from a list that was developed by a minister. He reviewed this list whenever he felt vulnerable to sexual temptation. He cited the following as a reminder of the negative consequences that a wrong moral choice could produce.[38]

- Grieving the Lord who redeemed me.

- Dragging His sacred name into the mud.

- One day having to look Jesus, the Righteous Judge, in the face and give an account for my actions.

- Following in the footsteps of those whose immorality forfeited or crippled their ministries and caused me to shudder: (list names)

- Inflicting untold hurt on my best friend, my loyal wife.

- Losing my wife's respect and trust.

- Hurting my beloved children.

- Destroying my example and credibility with my children and nullifying both present and future efforts to teach them to obey God ("Why listen to a man who betrayed Mom and us?").

- If my blindness should continue or my wife be unable to forgive, perhaps losing my wife and my children forever.

- Causing shame to my family ("Why isn't Daddy a pastor any more?").

- Losing self-respect.

- Creating a form of guilt awfully hard to shake. Even though God would forgive me, would I forgive myself?

- Forming memories and flashbacks that could plague future intimacy with my wife.

- Wasting years of ministry training and experience for a long time, maybe permanently.

---

[38] Alcorn, Randy, "Strategies To Keep From Falling," *Leadership Journal,* Winter 1988, 46.

- Forfeiting the effect of years of witnessing to other family members and reinforcing their distrust for ministers that has only begun to soften by my example, but that would harden, perhaps permanently, because of my immorality.

- Undermining the faithful example and hard work of other Christians in our community.

- Bringing great pleasure to Satan, the enemy of God and all that is good.

- Heaping judgment and endless difficulty on the person with whom I committed adultery.

- Possibly bearing the physical consequences of such diseases as gonorrhea, syphilis, chlamydia, herpes, and AIDS; perhaps infecting my wife, or in the case of AIDS, even causing her death.

- Possibly causing pregnancy, with all the personal and financial implications, including a lifelong reminder of my sin.

- Bringing hurt to these fellow pastors and elders: (list names).

- Causing shame and hurt to these friends, especially those I've led to Christ and discipled: (list names)

- Invoking shame and lifelong embarrassment upon myself.

It would be beneficial to every person who is in spiritual leadership (and every believer for that matter) to periodically go through the book of Proverbs and read about the dynamics and consequences that are involved in adultery. Some of the key warning passages for study and meditation include:

- Proverbs 2:16-19
- Proverbs 5:1-23
- Proverbs 6:20-35
- Proverbs 7:1-27
- Proverbs 9:13-18
- Proverbs 23:27-28
- Proverbs 31:1-3

At the beginning of Proverbs, we learn that these writings reflect a father's advice to his son. Of course, a mother's proverbs (advice) to her daughter would read differently. Young ladies need instructions and warnings about perils in relationships as well. Regardless of who is receiving the instruction, it is good to remember that, "Sin will take you further than you intended to go, keep you longer than you intended to stay, and cost you more than you intended to pay."

- **Recognize that moral failure does not begin with the physical act of adultery. Be conscious of and avoid precipitating factors.**

Spiritual leaders often provide care and comfort to hurting people. Sometimes this can create emotional bonds and even if intentions were innocent, the one receiving such ministry can find an emotional attraction and attachment forming toward the caregiver. Gratitude and appreciation that is expressed by the recipient can begin to feed the ego of the caregiver and begin to meet an emotional need in him. Consequently, this can develop into an unhealthy relationship.

"No pastor can long fail to notice the discrepancy between his wife's realistic appraisal of him as a husband and the lavish praise that fawning congregants shower on him as 'the godly minister.' When this occurs, the pastor is vulnerable to the temptation to transfer intimacy from his spouse to those who so uncritically feed his emotional needs."[39]

Adultery does not begin with the physical act. It begins with emotional camaraderie, flirtation, unchecked desires, fantasizing, rationalizing, justifying, violated boundaries, etc. Ministers need to avoid any type of flirtatious behavior, including playing with people's emotions. Be professional, and above all, be Christian!

---

[39]Grenz, Stanley J. and Bell, Roy D., *Betrayal of Trust*, (Grand Rapids: Baker Books, 2001), 50.

"You have heard the commandment that says, 'You must not commit adultery.' But I say, anyone who even looks at a woman with lust has already committed adultery with her in his heart. So if your eye—even your good eye—causes you to lust, gouge it out and throw it away. It is better for you to lose one part of your body than for your whole body to be thrown into hell. And if your hand—even your stronger hand—causes you to sin, cut it off and throw it away. It is better for you to lose one part of your body than for your whole body to be thrown into hell.

Matthew 5:27-30 (NLT)

You need to be brutally honest with yourself if you find yourself:

- Sensing an inappropriate attraction to a person other than your spouse.

- Thinking about a person, hoping to receive calls from that person, having fantasies about another person.

- Fabricating ways to legitimize a closer relationship with that person (e.g., appointing that person to a position in order to have more interaction).

- Communicating with or meeting that person in inappropriate ways or times, or in out-of-the-way places.

- Having thoughts about or communication with that person that you would not want your spouse to know about.

- **Establish and maintain proper boundaries for yourself in your life and ministry.**

This means having guidelines to follow that will keep you away from the edge. Here are some general guidelines:

- Don't counsel members of the opposite sex alone.

- Don't put yourself in a situation where, if an accusation were to arise, it would be your word against another's.

- Don't make house calls to a person of the opposite sex unless your spouse is with you or unless the spouse of the person you're going to visit is present.

- Don't use language that could be construed to mean more than what you intend to convey. Too much "chumminess" and inappropriate self-disclosure is beyond the scope of proper conduct.

- Don't touch people in ways that are inappropriate or could be misconstrued.

- **Be Accountable.**

Have someone you can talk with if you find yourself being tempted. Who are you accountable to? There should be someone (or more than one person) who is able to observe you in your ministry and express concerns about any problems they might see - someone you will listen to, and whose input you will respect. Those who are "Lone Rangers" are more susceptible than those who have proper principles of accountability at work in their life.

A few years ago, a pastor-friend of mine asked if I would be his accountability partner, relative to Internet usage. I agreed, on the condition that he would do the same for me. Both of us downloaded Internet accountability software and started receiving weekly reports of Internet sites that we visited. Sin loves to take advantage of secrecy and this type of accountability can be a strong deterrent to temptation.

Ephesians 5:13 (AMP) says, "But when anything is exposed and reproved by the light, it is made visible and clear; and where everything is visible and clear there is light."

Questions for Reflection and Discussion

1. How much do you feel that the cause of Christ has been hurt by immorality among His representatives and within the church?

_____

_____

_____

_____

_____

_____

2. How clear do you believe the Bible is concerning the moral conduct of believers and spiritual leaders? What decisions has this caused you to make, and what guidelines have you established for yourself to maintain moral purity in your life?_____

_____

_____

_____

_____

_____

_____

3. In this chapter concerning the painful consequences of immorality," a list was given that had been written by a minister. He used that list as a reminder any time he felt he might be tempted. As you reviewed that list, did any points in particular stand out to you? If so, which ones?

_____

_____

_____

_____

_____

_____

_____

4. What is the main insight that you have gained from this chapter?

_____

_____

_____

_____

_____

_____

_____

_____

_____

Chapter Seventeen

REFLECTIONS ON SCANDAL

"Those who teach by their doctrine must teach by their life, or else they pull down with one hand what they build up with the other."
- Matthew Henry

Key Thought: *Spiritual leaders need to realize that their decisions and actions are never "private" when they have the potential to bring great reproach upon the cause of Christ.*

What happens when scandal hits the church? What is the fallout? All believers, and especially those in positions of spiritual leadership and responsibility in the church, should often remind themselves of the significance of their witness.

King David created a world of hurt and problems when he committed adultery with Bathsheba (and then murdered Uriah in an attempted cover-up). David was forgiven of his sin, but there were still severe repercussions. The rest of David's life was beset with heartache and tragedy, and his reign was marked by one disaster after another.

Let's look at three after-effects from David's sin:

- **Nathan said, *"The sword shall never depart from your house"*** (2 Samuel 12:10). That's sobering! It's important to understand that spiritual forgiveness doesn't immediately eradicate all of the consequences of our actions. If I went out and robbed a bank tomorrow, I believe that God would forgive me; however, the courts probably wouldn't. Consequently, I would embarrass my family and destroy the trust that others have placed in me. Trust is the currency of ministry and without credibility, our ability to influence other people's lives is greatly diminished. Yes, David received forgiveness, but the ramifications that he experienced socially, relationally, and politically following his sin were massive, horrific, and long-term.

- **God did not look at David's sin as merely yielding to temptation; it was much deeper than that in God's eyes.** In reference to David's act of disobedience, God said, "...you have despised me..." (2 Samuel 12:10). God takes our obedience (and our disobedience) very seriously and very personally. Jesus said, "If you love me, keep my commandments" (John 14:15). God is never impressed with our words if our actions are wrong. First John 2:4 states, "He who says, 'I know Him,' and does not keep His commandments, is a liar, and the truth is not in him." Before there was a "Great Commission," there was a "Great Commandment," which involves loving the Lord our God with all of our heart, soul, mind, and strength. Real love for God produces obedience to Him.

- **Another very sobering statement is, *"...by this deed you have given great occasion to the enemies of the LORD to blaspheme..."*** (2 Samuel 12:14). We know that the Gospel is true, whether a particular minister lives right or not; however, society, as a whole, tends to judge the message by the messenger. When Paul spoke of those who preach one thing and live another (Romans 2:21-24), he ended those remarks with, "For the name of God is blasphemed among the Gentiles because of you."

Beginning in Matthew 18:6, Jesus talks about offenses, and He addresses the serious consequences of offending "one of these little ones." The words translated "offend" and "offense" (used six times in these few verses), are *skandalizo* and *scandaloon* in the Greek. This is where we get our English word, scandal.

Scandalous behavior by Christians brings offense and causes people to stumble. It disheartens and confuses baby Christians, alienates those who may have been considering Christianity, and gives great occasion to the enemies of the Lord to blaspheme.

What I am writing is not meant to project condemnation toward anyone who has failed in the past. We are called to be proponents of mercy and restoration (Galatians 6:1, James 5:19-20). I am simply summarizing what was a stark reminder to me of the seriousness of our calling and the mandate that we must embrace regarding godly living if we are going to preach the Gospel effectively. This is not a time to rise up in judgment against others; it is a time to examine our own hearts in godly fear.

Warnings against sin go way back. When Cain was angry and jealous toward Abel, God said, "You will be accepted if you do what is right. But if you refuse to do what is right, then watch out! Sin is crouching at the door, eager to control you. But you must subdue it and be its master" (Genesis 4:7, NLT).

Even Paul, as spiritually developed as he was, didn't trust his flesh. He said, "But I discipline my body and bring it into subjection, lest, when I have preached to others, I myself should become disqualified" (1 Corinthians 9:27). Spurgeon's words also ring true yet today: "Whatever 'call' a man may pretend to have, if he has not been called to holiness, he certainly has not been called to the ministry."[40]

Someone described the deceptive and destructive power of sin this way: "Sin will take you farther than you want to go! Sin will keep you longer than you want to stay! Sin will cost you more than you want to pay!"

Saying "No," Saying "Yes"

I believe that our destinies are formed more by the choices we make than by the circumstances we encounter. Our character and future are shaped, for the most part, by what we say "No" to, and what we say "Yes" to.

- Abraham said "No" to Sodom's riches, and "Yes" to God's promises.

- Joseph said "No" to Potiphar's wife, and "Yes" to faithful service.

- Moses said "No" to the treasures of Egypt, and "Yes" to a heavenly assignment.

- Elisha said "No" to Naaman's silver, and "Yes" to selfless integrity.

- Daniel said "No" to the king's delicacies, and "Yes" to godly consecration.

- Nehemiah said "No" to compromising negotiations, and "Yes" to unwavering persistence.

- Paul said "No" to being burdensome to the churches, and "Yes" to sacrificial love.

- Jesus said "No" to comfort, and "Yes" to the cross.

---

[40]Spurgeon, C.H., *Lectures to My Students*, (Grand Rapids: Zondervan, 1954), 9.

Jesus expected us to have a strong "Yes" and a clear "No." Both He and James said, "...let your 'Yes ' be 'Yes,' and your 'No,' 'No.'" If we find ourselves torn or tempted when it comes to doing the right thing, it's important that we go back to our core values and remind ourselves who God has called us to be. Roy Disney said, "It's not hard to make decisions when you know what your values are."

Questions for Reflection and Discussion

1. Why would David still have experienced negative consequences from his sin with Bathsheba if God had forgiven him? Does spiritual forgiveness automatically remove the ramifications of our actions in all areas?

_____

_____

_____

_____

_____

_____

_____

2. Once again in this chapter, the phrase, "Trust is the currency of ministry" was used. What does this mean to you?_____

_____

_____

_____

_____

_____

_____

3. Can a believer who chooses to sin be more than just yielding to temptation? What biblical grounds do we have to say that?_____

_____

_____

_____

_____

_____

_____

_____

_____

4. What is the main insight that you gained from this chapter?

_____

_____

_____

_____

_____

_____

_____

_____

MINISTRY KILLERS YOU MUST CONQUER– THE GLORY

Chapter Eighteen

EGO AND PRIDE ISSUES

"A man's pride will bring him low, but the humble in spirit will retain honor."

- Proverbs 29:23

Key Thought: *Spiritual leaders must be aware of and guard themselves against the intoxicating and devastating influence of pride, especially when experiencing "success."*

Pride is insidious. It deceives the one infected, causing him to think "more" of himself, and "less" of God.

- Pride was a major factor in Lucifer's downfall. Ezekiel 28:17 says, "Your heart was lifted up because of your beauty." The result of this pride? "...you have said in your heart: 'I will ascend into heaven, I will exalt my throne above the stars of God'" (Isaiah 14:13).

- The Apostle Paul taught that a novice was not to be appointed as a bishop, "...lest being puffed up with pride he fall into the same condemnation as the devil" (1 Timothy 3:6).

- Before King Saul became prideful, arrogant, and disobedient, Samuel referred to an earlier time: "When you were small in your own sight, were you not made the head of the tribes of Israel, and the Lord anointed you king over Israel?" (1 Samuel 15:17, AMP).

- King Uzziah fell into pride after God had given him success. "...He did what was right in the sight of the LORD... and as long as he sought the LORD, God made him prosper. So his fame spread far and wide, for he was marvelously helped till he became strong. But when he was strong his heart was lifted up, to his destruction" (2 Chronicles 26:4-5, 15-16).

- Proverbs 16:18 says, "Pride goes before destruction, and a haughty spirit before a fall."

- James 4:6 and 1 Peter 5:5 both say, "God resists the proud, but gives grace to the humble."

Others have observed the connection between power, success, and pride. In 1887, Lord Acton wrote, "Power tends to corrupt, and absolute power corrupts absolutely." Before that, Abraham Lincoln had said, "Nearly all men can stand adversity, but if you want to test a man's character, give him power." Gifted British author and Bible teacher, Donald Gee, said, "Any burst of popularity and success calls for a disciplined personality to sustain it untarnished. It can easily spell spiritual ruin. It takes a steady hand to carry a full cup." [41]

Gordon Lindsay's ministry allowed him to witness the rise and fall of many prominent ministers during the Pentecostal and healing revivals in America. He noted, "Some spiritual moves have been blessed of God, and then suddenly have faded away because of the presumptuous and

---

[41] Gee, Donald, *A Way to Escape.* (Springfield, MO: Gospel Publishing House, Reprint 1966), 61.

erratic conduct of certain leaders. One such move occurred some years ago in America. At first we rejoiced in this outpouring of the Spirit. But very soon we saw something develop that alarmed us. Some of the leaders were claiming that they were the 'Powerhouse' and all other churches were 'dried up.' They said that people should come to them to get recharged. When we saw such bold pretensions, we realized that the usefulness of such leaders could not last long." [42]

Elsewhere, Lindsay wrote, "Certain men of God, once mightily used of the Lord were not able to stand prosperity, but became erratic and inconsistent in their conduct, and in the end passed from the scene under a cloud, and some even in disgrace. The human ego, unchecked, can only lead to one sad end—abasement and shame. This is God's universe, and He will not share His glory with fleshly ambition. Spiritual security may be found only in humility." [43]

Robert Foster said, "When we make ourselves more than nothing, we make God less than everything." [44]   Similarly, Andrew Murray noted, "As long as we are something, God cannot be all." [45]

How Is Pride Revealed in Spiritual Leadership?

- **Taking Credit for God's Grace.**

Bernard of Clairvaux said, "Pride causes us to use our gifts as though they came from ourselves, not benefits received from God, and to usurp our benefactor's glory." [46]

---

[42] Lindsay, Gordon, *God's 20th Century Barnabas*. (Dallas, TX: Christ for the Nations, Reprinted 1982), 277-278.

[43] Lindsay, Gordon, "Seven Dangers the Church Faces Today." *The Voice of Healing*, September, 1951.

[44] Bob Kelly, Editor. *Worth Repeating*, (Grand Rapids: Kregel Publications, 2003), 306.

[45] ibid, page 307.

[46] Water, Mark, *The New Encyclopedia of Christian Quotations*, (Grand Rapids: Baker Books, 2000), 828

The Lord Jesus Christ lived and ministered in total reliance on the Father. He said:

- *"I can do nothing on my own. ...I carry out the will of the one who sent me, not my own will"* (John 5:30, NLT).

- *"The words I speak are not my own, but my Father who lives in me does his work through me"* (John 14:10, NLT).

If Jesus, in humility, was completely dependent on the Father for all that was accomplished through His ministry, what would make us think that we could accomplish anything apart from Him? Paul asked a very powerful question to believers in Corinth: "What do you have that God hasn't given you? And if everything you have is from God, why boast as though it were not a gift?" (1 Corinthians 4:7, NLT).

In his second epistle to the same church, Paul shared his perspective of his own ministry: "It is not that we think we are qualified to do anything on our own. Our qualification comes from God. He has enabled us to be ministers of his new covenant" (2 Corinthians 3:5-6, NLT). Charles Spurgeon wisely said, "Be not proud of race, face, place, or grace." Always remember that the gifts God has given you are for His glory and for the purpose of blessing others.

- If God has given you the gift of teaching, it is so others can learn.

- If God has given you the gift of pastoring, it is so others can be cared for.

- If God has given you the gift of evangelism, it is so the lost can be saved.

Never take glory unto yourself for what God has given you or for how God uses you! Humble ministers not only recognize the absolute necessity of the ability of God at work in their lives, but they also recognize the valuable contributions of other people who work with them and for them. They are quick to give credit to others and to show gratitude for the service of others.

- **Carnal Ambition**

Much of what we have said previously implies that pride is most likely to be a problem after a person has experienced great success, but there is also a form of pride that can precede any kind of achievements. Before their ministries were ever launched, pride caused the disciples to clamor among themselves, arguing about which of them would be the greatest. Jesus had to break up arguments among them as they jockeyed for position and strove for prominence.

> *So Jesus got them together to settle things down. He said, "You've observed how godless rulers throw their weight around, how quickly a little power goes to their heads. It's not going to be that way with you. Whoever wants to be great must become a servant. Whoever wants to be first among you must be your slave. That is what the Son of Man has done: He came to serve, not be served—and then to give away his life..."*
> Matthew 20:25-28 (MSG)

Jesus made it clear that His Kingdom was not going to be based on dog-eat-dog politics or the "get-ahead-at-any-cost" system of the world. In God's Kingdom, it is His responsibility to call, appoint, and promote; it is man's responsibility to serve.

Oswald Sanders said, "The word 'ambition' comes from a Latin word meaning 'campaigning for promotion.' The phrase suggests a variety of elements: social visibility and approval, popularity, peer recognition, the exercise of authority over others. Ambitious people, in this sense, enjoy the power that comes with money and authority. Jesus had no time for such ego-driven ambitions. The true spiritual leader will never 'campaign for promotion.'"[47]

What would carnal ambition look like in the life of a spiritual leader?

- Wanting to be noticed

- Posturing to make oneself look important

- Competing against, instead of cooperating with others

- Self-exaltation

- Trying to make "oneself" look good, even if that means making others look bad

- Engaged in power plays

- Positions are a power trip, not opportunities to serve

The Apostle John spoke of one church leader named Diotrephes, "... who loves to have the preeminence" (3 John 9). Paul spoke of another group that was busy "politicking" against him by trying to defame and undermine him. "Those people are zealous to win you over, but for no good. What they want is to alienate you [from us], so that you may be zealous for them" (Galatians 4:17, NIV).

Jesus described the attitude that He wants His servant-leaders to have.

"When you are invited to a wedding feast, don't sit in the seat of honor. What if someone who is more distinguished than you has also been invited? The host will come and say, 'Give this person your seat.' Then you will be embarrassed, and you will have to take whatever seat is left at the foot of the table! Instead, take the lowest place at the foot of the

---

[47]Sanders, Oswald, *Spiritual Leadership*. (Chicago: Moody Press, 1994), 15.

table. Then when your host sees you, he will come and say, 'Friend, we have a better place for you!' Then you will be honored in front of all the other guests. For those who exalt themselves will be humbled, and those who humble themselves will be exalted.

Luke 14:8-11 (NLT)

- **Self-Centeredness**

"The counterfeit trinity is me, myself, and I."[48]

- Edwin Louis Cole

Years ago, a pastor told me, "The Lord showed me that anyone who starts a church within 50 miles of mine is out of the will of God." I was shocked that anyone could have such an exclusive, territorial mentality - but pride will create a distorted mindset.

Have you ever met people who were so self-focused that in conversation and in preaching, everything related back to them instead of to God or God's people. If you were telling them about something that happened to you, they were quick to interrupt with, "That reminds of the time that I..." Someone said, "Conceit is the only disease known to man that makes everyone sick except the one who has it."

What are some of the other traits of self-centeredness?

- Thinking that God's eternal plan revolves around me

- Acting like ours is the only true work of God in town

- Believing that what God does through others is less significant than what He does through me

- Being obsessed with one's own image

---

[48]Cole, Edwin Louis, *Strong Men in Tough Times*, (Southlake, TX: Watercolor Books, 1993), 34.

God has called us to bless, not to impress. Our ministries are supposed to be an expression of the Lord's goodness, not an extension of our egos.

- **An Attitude of Superiority**

If leaders develop a superiority complex, they begin to feel they are above criticism and reproach. They are quick to jump behind the defense of "Touch not God's anointed," instead of humbly facing what could be justifiable criticism.

Through inappropriate conduct, some leaders may actually be promoting and fueling the complaints that, by their very authority, they are trying to suppress. Certain leaders feel they should never be questioned: "Don't question anything I say or do. What I say and do is right, because I am God's man!" Such a presumptuous sense of infallibility is a sure indicator that pride has brought great blindness.

Leaders who deem themselves superior may demand absolute and exclusive reign over the flock: "Don't listen to anyone but me!" They may use the phrase, "The Lord told me..." to get their way, and in extreme cases, to even justify unethical, immoral, or illegal conduct.

Other indicators of an attitude of superiority:

- A sense of infallibility ("I'm never wrong; I'm always right.")

- "My preferences = God's directives."

- "I've got a greater anointing... greater revelation..."

- The success of others is minimized because they are obviously compromising (or are invalidated in some other way).

- "We are deeper than everyone else."

- An attitude of entitlement, ("I deserve whatever I want because of who I am.")

- Unwillingness to be accountable or to receive correction.

Spiritual leaders must avoid surrounding themselves with "yes men" who feed their ego and offer unrelenting praise. I know of one leader who deemed anyone who said anything positive about him, to have been sent from God. Likewise, anyone who said anything that seemed the least bit negative was believed to have been sent from the devil.

Norman Vincent Peale said, "The trouble with most of us is that we would rather be ruined by praise than saved by criticism." Similar wisdom was expressed long before in Proverbs 27:6, "Faithful are the wounds of a friend, but the kisses of an enemy are deceitful."

- **The Absence of a Servant's Heart**

Jesus made it clear in His ministry that He had not come to be served, but to serve (Matthew 20:28). If we forget that and begin to act like others are here to serve us, then we have made more of ourselves than Jesus made of Himself.

Don't be selfish; don't try to impress others. Be humble, thinking of others as better than yourselves. Don't look out only for your own interests, but take an interest in others, too. You must have the same attitude that Christ Jesus had. Though he was God, he did not think of equality with God as something to cling to. Instead, he gave up his divine privileges; he took the humble position of a slave and was born as a human being. When he appeared in human form, he humbled himself in obedience to God and died a criminal's death on a cross.

Philippians 2:3-8 (NLT)

Those of us who are strong and able in the faith need to step in and lend a hand to those who falter, and not just do what is most convenient for us. Strength is for service, not status.

Romans 15:1 (MSG)

God's servants must keep themselves from having a "celebrity" mentality. God wants those who lead to be servants, not celebrities.

• Disregard for Others

Spiritual leaders should be courteous, polite, respectful, and appreciative of others. They should not be "respecters of persons," treating people of high standing with respect, while treating others in a condescending manner. Romans 12:16 (MSG) says, "Get along with each other; don't be stuck-up. Make friends with nobodies; don't be the great somebody." The NLT renders the middle part of that verse, "Don't be too proud to enjoy the company of ordinary people."

If you want to know something about the character of a person, then watch how they treat people they deem to be in so-called "lesser" positions. They may be very respectful to the boss or a person of high status, but how do they treat the janitor, a waitress, a sales clerk, or a secretary? There is simply no place for rudeness or haughtiness in the life of a spiritual leader.

If a leader perceives himself as being superior to others, then it is likely that he will mistreat and disrespect others. He will see them merely as a means to fulfill his own goals. In short, people will end up being used. Spiritual leaders need to draw a distinct line between motivating people versus manipulating people. Healthy motivation does not take place through guilt, fear or intimidation.

Spiritual leaders encourage others to serve in healthy ways with appropriate boundaries. They don't want people to serve at the expense of their families or their health. "Give 'til it hurts" is the motto of some leaders, and "hurt" is exactly what their ministries produce. In the wake of these ministries, you will find many hurting and wounded people.

- **Grandiosity**

Pride will also surface in a type of grandiosity that produces a "one-upsmanship" mentality in one's leadership. Everything is exaggerated. Numbers are stretched to make the leader look good. Stories are embellished. Name dropping is done regularly in an attempt to establish a glowing reputation and to boost one's ego.

When grandiosity is present, truth is secondary to image-projection and image-maintenance. Professionals in various fields have been known to "doctor" their resumes, in an attempt to enhance their image. Some preachers have personalized generic illustrations while preaching, presenting the story as though it was their story. Such deceptiveness is always a violation of personal integrity, and when discovered, damages a leader's credibility.

A Word of Caution

There is certainly a bona fide way of exercising authority in legitimate spiritual leadership. There are times when leaders need to take a strong stand and deal firmly with certain situations; this does not make him a dictator or a tyrant.

A godly leader is not a doormat to be trampled upon by disgruntled "saints" or a piñata to be beaten by unruly congregants. Spiritual leadership is not found in the lack of authority, but in the proper use of authority. Even when Paul was dealing with conflict, he told believers, "I want to use the authority the Lord has given me to strengthen you, not to tear you down" (2 Corinthians 13:10, NLT).

This should be the heart-cry of every person in spiritual leadership. We lead to benefit those whom we have the privilege of serving. Our leadership should build, benefit, and bless others. Pride is a ministry killer, that is diametrically opposed to God's nature and His plan for our lives.

Questions for Reflection and Discussion

1. What does Spurgeon's statement ("Be not proud of race, face, place, or grace") mean to you?_____

_____

_____

_____

_____

_____

_____

_____

_____

2. Have you ever recognized pride in your own life? How was pride expressed, how did you come to recognize it as such, and how did you deal with that issue in your life?_____

_____

_____

_____

_____

_____

_____

3. Norman Vincent Peale said, "The trouble with most of us is that we would rather be ruined by praise than saved by criticism." Have you been able to filter through your emotional reaction toward criticism in some situation and see there was some truth there that you needed to act upon?

_____

_____

_____

_____

_____

_____

_____

_____

_____

_____

4. What do you think Paul meant when he said you must have the same attitude that Christ Jesus had? What guidelines does that provide for us?

_____

_____

_____

_____

_____

_____

_____

_____

_____

_____

_____

5. What is the main insight that you have gained from this chapter?

_____

_____

_____

_____

_____

_____

_____

_____

_____

_____

_____

_____

_____

_____

_____

Chapter Nineteen

WEAK
LEADERS

"God creates out of nothing. Therefore, until a man is nothing, God can make nothing out of him."

- Martin Luther

Key Point: *Greatness in spiritual leadership is not found in exerting your strength, but by discovering His strength through your weakness.*

There's a lot to be said for strength. Given the choice, I think most everyone would say that they prefer strength over weakness. Everyone wants their health to be strong, their financial portfolio to be strong, their marriage and family to be strong, their church to be strong, etc.

There are also many great Scriptures about being strong. Joshua was commanded six times to "Be strong and of good courage." Paul admonished the Ephesians to "be strong in the Lord and in the power of His might" (Ephesians 6:10) and he charged his young protégé, Timothy, to "be strong in the grace that is in Christ Jesus" (2 Timothy 2:1).

Avoiding the Counterfeit

There is also a counterfeit strength that can masquerade as the authentic. Only genuine strength—that which is rooted in the grace of God—will stand the test of time. Counterfeit expressions of strength include:

- arrogance

- bravado

- projecting an air of self-importance or an attitude of superiority

- posturing

- haughtiness

- intimidation

These may produce certain results for a season, but they will ultimately crumble and fail.

Paul was speaking of counterfeit strength when he facetiously said that he was "too weak" to engage in a type of leadership that he deemed to be abusive and manipulative of people. He was expressing concern over the gullibility of the Corinthians when he said, "For you put up with it if one brings you into bondage, if one devours you, if one takes from you, if one exalts himself, if one strikes you on the face. To our shame I say that we were too weak for that!" (2 Corinthians 11:20-21).

Believers, and especially leaders, can sense pressure to present themselves exclusively in a positive light—to project the image that "I've got it all together and I'm large and in charge." Such facades are often superficial veneers for deep-rooted insecurity. To honestly acknowledge one's weakness or inability can seem to be a violation of making and maintaining a "good confession."

Finding the Genuine

So how do we find the genuine strength that God wants us to experience? It begins with acknowledging our own limitations. Only then will we be able to identify and possess true strength. Paul was a strong leader, but he was profoundly aware of his weaknesses. Consider Paul's statements that reflect his transparency and his high level of self-awareness:

- *"I was with you in weakness, in fear, and in much trembling"* (1 Corinthians 2:3).

- *"Therefore I take pleasure in infirmities, in reproaches, in needs, in persecutions, in distresses, for Christ's sake. For when I am weak, then I am strong"* (2 Corinthians 12:10).

- *"For we also are weak in Him, but we shall live with Him by the power of God toward you"* (2 Corinthians 13:4).

- *"...to the weak I became as weak, that I might win the weak"* (1 Corinthians 9:22).

- *"Who is weak, and I am not weak?"* (2 Corinthians 11:29).

- *"for in nothing was I behind the most eminent apostles, though I am nothing"* (2 Corinthians 12:11).

While these scriptures need to be qualified and read in context, there's no doubt that Paul was not full of himself or flippantly self-assured. He put no confidence in the flesh (Philippians 3:3). He also said, "...we had the sentence of death in ourselves, that we should not trust in ourselves but in God who raises the dead" (2 Corinthians 1:9).

Paul was not consumed with his accomplishments or the fact that he had started a certain number of churches or that he had "cutting-edge" revelation from God. Rather, he was humbled by an assignment that he knew he could never accomplish on his own, and he realized that he was utterly and completely dependent on God's ability.

Smith Wigglesworth said: "I believe that God wants to put His hand upon us so that we may reach ideal definitions of humility, of human helplessness, of human insufficiency, until we will rest no more upon human plans, but have God's thoughts, God's voice, and the Holy Spirit to speak to us."[49]

Jesus said, "I can of Myself do nothing" (John 5:30). The Amplified version of that verse reads: "I am able to do nothing from Myself [independently, of My own accord — but only as I am taught by God and as I get His orders]." If anyone could have ever rightly trusted in Himself or have felt self-sufficient, it was Jesus, and yet He utterly and entirely relied upon God. He did not carry Himself in a haughty manner in order to impress others. Rather, He was "gentle and lowly of heart" (Matthew 11:29).

Not only did Jesus exemplify absolute reliance upon God, but He also let us know that we needed the same sense of dependence. He said in John 15:5, "...for without Me you can do nothing."

So if You Feel a Little Weak...

To me, this is one of the most liberating truths that we can embrace! We don't have to prove to anyone how wonderful we are, how perfect we are, or how spiritual we are. This is not an invitation to sloppy living or an excuse for not growing, but it enables us to know that God accepts us unconditionally and chose us in spite of our "imperfect-ness."

If you feel weak, that's okay, because:

---

[49]Patricia Culbertson, Editor, *Smith Wigglesworth Devotional,* (New Kensington, PA: Whitaker House, 1999), 256.

- *"God has chosen the weak things of the world to put to shame the things which are mighty"* (2 Corinthians 1:27).

- *"He gives power to the weak, and to those who have no might He increases strength"* (Isaiah 40:29).

- *"My strength comes into its own in your weakness"* (2 Corinthians 12:9, MSG).

- Of the Old Testament heroes of faith, we read, *"They were weak, and yet were made strong. They were powerful in battle and defeated other armies"* (Hebrews 11:34, NCV).

It takes a very secure person to acknowledge his weakness and to rely totally on God's strength. It's the kind of child-like faith that is expressed in the words of the song that so many of us learned at a very young age: *"Little ones to Him belong; they are weak, but He is strong."* We have to become comfortable with our inadequacy and His adequacy. I pray that you will be comfortable in your weakness and confident in His strength!

Questions for Reflection and Discussion

1. Paul made several statements indicating an awareness of his weakness. Why do you think Paul made so many statements about his deficiencies, and how did he have such a powerful ministry in spite of those weaknesses?

_____

_____

_____

_____

_____

_____

2. There are many biblical admonitions to "be strong," yet even Jesus said that He was "gentle and lowly of heart." How can a Christian be weak and strong at the same time?_____

_____

_____

_____

_____

_____

_____

3. Have you ever sensed a need to present yourself as being strong in a way that could have been perceived as bravado or even arrogance? If so, what was the motivation and purpose behind doing that?_____

_____

_____

_____

_____

_____

_____

4. What is the main insight that you have gained from this chapter?

_____

_____

_____

_____

_____

_____

_____

Chapter Twenty

GURUS, GROUPIES, AND GULLIBILITY

"We're not in charge of how you live out the faith, looking over your shoulders, suspiciously critical. We're partners, working alongside you, joyfully expectant. I know that you stand by your own faith, not by ours."

- 2 Corinthians 1:24 (MSG)

Key Thought: *Spiritual leaders do not cultivate a dependency in others upon themselves; they teach others to think biblically and to rely upon the Holy Spirit.*

I f you are my age or a bit older, you may remember the hysteria surrounding the Beatles when they first became popular. In addition to *"Let It Be"* and *"I Want to Hold Your Hand,"* you may recall "teeny-bopper" fans, who were beside themselves: screaming, crying, and swooning in their presence.

This phenomenon of being caught up and carried away in a frenzy of unthinking enthusiasm is not restricted to teenage girls and rock stars. Sometimes it is far more sinister with deadly results. Adolf Hitler said, "What luck for rulers that men do not think." One of Hitler's leading henchmen, Herman Goering said, "I have no conscience. Adolf Hitler is my conscience."[50] The ability and courage to think clearly in the context of truth is essential if one is to avoid being deceived in large or small matters.

The word "gullible" is thought to have been derived from "gull" - the bird. The words "gull" and "gullet" refer to swallowing and the throat. Gulls (as in seagulls) were said to swallow anything that was thrown at them. Likewise, a gullible person is easily deceived, accepting the thoughts of others without intelligent consideration as to their veracity.

Believers sometimes become enamored with certain charismatic leaders and blindly embrace every word they say, putting them on pedestals and forgetting all of the Bible's admonitions about our need to operate with keen discernment and scriptural intelligence. Not only does it take spiritual insight to discern the truth, but it also takes courage to stand up for the truth and not be swept away with the swooning masses. It is important to remember that not everything that is popular is principled.

In the foreward of *Bonhoeffer: Pastor, Martyr, Prophet, Spy*, Timothy J. Keller addresses the capitulation of the German church to Hitler. "How could 'the church of Luther,' that great teacher of the gospel, have ever come to such a place? The answer is that the true gospel, summed up by Bonhoeffer as costly grace, had been lost. On the one hand, the church had become marked by formalism. That meant going to church and hearing that God just loves and forgives everyone, so it doesn't really matter much how you live. Bonhoeffer called this 'cheap grace.' On the other hand, there was legalism, or salvation by law and good works. Legalism meant that God loves you because you have pulled yourself together and are trying to live a good, disciplined life."[51]

---

[50]Fest, Joachim E., *The Face of the Third Reich: Portraits of the Nazi Leadership*, (Boston: Da Capo Press, 1970) 75.

[51]Metaxas, Eric, *Bonhoeffer*, (Nashville: Thomas Nelson, 2010), Foreword.

Bonhoeffer demonstrated what it meant to be an independent thinker. Educated in the midst of extreme theological liberalism, he defied many of the academic giants of his day, and later actively withstood the evils of Nazism as well. I admire his courage and the deliberateness of his thought processes.

Bonhoeffer's independence reminds me of Paul's tenacity and stand for the truth in the light of what he saw in the church at Antioch. Galatians 2:11-13 says, "But when Peter came to Antioch, I had to oppose him to his face, for what he did was very wrong. When he first arrived, he ate with the Gentile Christians, who were not circumcised. But afterward, when some friends of James came, Peter wouldn't eat with the Gentiles anymore. He was afraid of criticism from these people who insisted on the necessity of circumcision. As a result, other Jewish Christians followed Peter's hypocrisy, and even Barnabas was led astray by their hypocrisy."

Peter and Barnabas were no doubt good men, but in this unfortunate moment, they became "groupies" who were simply following the crowd. In this particular situation, they lacked the insight and/or the fortitude to stand up for what was right.

The Bible stresses the need to not be gullible, but to use study, wisdom, and discernment in our lives.

The gullible believe anything they're told; the prudent sift and weigh every word.

Proverbs 14:15 (MSG)

I want you also to be smart, making sure every "good" thing is the real thing. Don't be gullible in regard to smooth-talking evil. Stay alert like this...

Romans 16:19 (MSG)

But I fear that somehow your pure and undivided devotion to Christ will be corrupted, just as Eve was deceived by the cunning ways of the serpent. You happily put up with whatever anyone tells you, even if they preach a different Jesus than the one we preach, or a different kind of Spirit than the one you received, or a different kind of gospel than the one you believed.

2 Corinthians 11:3-4 (NLT)

But test and prove all things [until you can recognize] what is good; [to that] hold fast.

1 Thessalonians 5:21 (AMP)

Beloved, do not believe every spirit, but test the spirits, whether they are of God; because many false prophets have gone out into the world.

1 John 4:1

Not only does all of this involve knowing the Bible and being led by the Holy Spirit, but it also involves a skill known as "critical thinking." A few of the many definitions of critical thinking include:

- *"Critical thinking is reasonable, reflective thinking that is focused on deciding what to believe and do."*

- *"...interpreting, analyzing, evaluating, and synthesizing information to form a good understanding, judgment, or solution."*

- *"...an ability to evaluate information and opinions in a systematic, purposeful, efficient manner."*

Being a critical thinker does not mean that you are a critical person. We typically think of critical in the sense of someone who is always negative, griping, tearing others down, etc. However, this is not what we're saying. Neither does critical thinking mean that you are narrow-minded or unwilling to consider other points of view.

I remember a spiritual leader sharing about a time when he was listening to another minister preach, and he recalled that he disagreed with some of the things the minister had said. Instead of shutting him off because of a disagreement, the spiritual leader continued listening (even though he was filtering as he listened), and later, said this minister communicated an outstanding truth that answered a question he had been wondering about for years. He said he was so glad that he didn't shut that minister off just because he had said some things earlier in the message that he disagreed with.

Job 34:3 says, "The ear tests the words it hears just as the mouth distinguishes between foods."

While we must be careful not to exalt our reasoning above God and His Word, God wants us to use our minds (guided by His Word and Spirit) in discerning truth. In Isaiah 1:18, God said, "Come now, and let us reason together..." Notice that we are supposed to reason with God, not to reason against Him. Logic and reason certainly are not our gods, but they are tools to be used in establishing our beliefs and practices. This is why Paul said, "Study and be eager and do your utmost to present yourself to God approved (tested by trial), a workman who has no cause to be ashamed, correctly analyzing and accurately dividing [rightly handling and skillfully teaching] the Word of Truth" (2 Timothy 2:15, AMP).

As leaders, God has not called us to be gurus. As followers, God has not called us to be groupies. And God has certainly not called any of us to be gullible. May God help us all as we seek to discern, embrace, and proclaim truth.

Questions for Reflection and Discussion

1. How do you feel you are in the area of gullibility? Do you believe you have a healthy balance of respect toward others, without failing to think scripturally for yourself? Are you like a Berean who, "...received the word with all readiness, and searched the Scriptures daily to find out whether these things were so" (Acts 17:11)?_____

_____

_____

_____

_____

_____

_____

_____

_____

_____

2. Do you encourage others to learn to think biblically for themselves? Do you encourage others not to be overly dependent on you?_____

_____

_____

_____

_____

_____

_____

_____

_____

_____

3. Do you avoid putting other people on pedestals? Do you discourage others from putting you on a pedestal?_____

_____

_____

_____

_____

_____

_____

_____

_____

_____

4. What is the main insight that you have gained from this chapter?_____

_____

_____

_____

_____

_____

_____

_____

_____

_____

_____

_____

_____

Chapter Twenty-One

TRAITS OF
SPIRITUAL FATHERS

"For the children ought not to lay up for the parents, but the parents for the children."

- 2 Corinthians 12:14

Key Thought: *True spiritual fathers seek the welfare and betterment of those they serve.*

A few years ago, when I was preparing to teach at an overseas ministers' conference, the host missionary asked if I could teach not only on "How to be a Timothy," but also along the lines of "How to be a Paul." He explained that there was a significant rift in his country between spiritual "fathers" and spiritual "sons."

He said that some "sons" were getting trained and then undermining the pastors and splitting their churches. In addition, some pastors were fearful of such uprisings and ran off any "sons" who seemed to have ministerial potential before such problems could arise. There were problems on both ends.

I've also heard of situations in which so-called spiritual fathers have offered their services (for a price), but it seems questionable as to whether their efforts were really directed toward the development and progress of the sons, or if they were merely creating a self-promoting hierarchy and cultivating the sons' loyalties to themselves. I can't imagine Paul endorsing a "rent-a-dad" approach to ministry!

Still, legitimate and healthy father-son relationships are important. Dr. Howard Hendricks said there are "...three kinds of mentoring relationships that a man desperately needs to pursue: a Paul, an older man who can build into his life; a Barnabas, a peer, a soul brother to whom he can be accountable; and a Timothy, a younger man into whose life he is building." [52]

Paul was a spiritual father not only to Timothy and Titus, but also to churches as well. Paul sometimes referred to himself in a "fathering-type" of role, and he articulated certain characteristics that he exhibited toward those to whom he ministered. What do we see in these passages about the heart of a spiritual father?

- He did not flatter them (1 Thessalonians 2:5). He wasn't buttering them up just so they'd like him or so that he could get something out of them.

- He was not covetous toward them (1 Thessalonians 2:5). He didn't see having a relationship with them as a means of getting their goods.

- He did not seek the glory of men – he wasn't seeking to be exalted (1 Thessalonians 2:6). This wasn't about Paul gathering sons around him to feed his own ego.

- He was not demanding of them. He wasn't controlling, manipulative, or dictatorial (1 Thessalonians 2:6).

- He exhibited a heart-felt, compassionate concern for their well-being.

---

[52]Hendricks, Howard, *As Iron Sharpens Iron,* (Chicago, IL: Moody Publishers, 1995), 78.

- He was gentle toward them (1 Thessalonians 2:7).

- He cherished them (1 Thessalonians 2:7).

- He longed for them affectionately (1 Thessalonians 2:8)

- He not only gave them the gospel, but he gave his own life to them (1 Thessalonians 2:8).

- They were dear to him (1 Thessalonians 2:8).

- He exhorted, comforted, and charged every one of them, as a father does his children (1 Thessalonians 2:11).

- His energies and efforts went toward their spiritual development (Galatians 4:19).

- He was not interested in shaming them, but did feel obligated to warn them. He wasn't putting them on a guilt trip or making them feel intimidated (1 Corinthians 4:14).

- He was different than a mere teacher – he wasn't just passing information on to them, but he had "begotten them" through the Gospel and was setting an example they could follow in their spiritual development (1 Corinthians 4:15-16).

- He wasn't seeking what was theirs (their money), but he was seeking them (2 Corinthians 12:14).

- He was willing to spend and be spent for them – in other words, he was willing to live and give sacrificially for them – for their advancement and their development (2 Corinthians 12:15).

If you are a mature leader, I pray that these are the traits that you will exhibit toward those whom you have the privilege of influencing. If you are in search of a father-figure, a mentor, or a role model in ministry, I trust you will keep these traits in mind as you look for someone who can be a good influence and example for you.

In closing, let me share one minister's quest to glean from some mentors. Many years ago, a good friend of mine (Pastor Gerald Brooks) realized that he needed more development in his life and ministry, so he sought some mentoring from a more seasoned minister. His attempt was not warmly received, so he set out to get some mentoring in the best way he knew how. He identified three Christian leaders that he admired and noted the distinct strengths that each one of them had.

Even though he didn't know any of these men personally, he got as many of their books and teaching tapes as he could. For years, he studied these men's writings and teachings to glean as much as possible. From one, he focused on learning spiritual and biblical truth; from the second, he zeroed in on learning pastoral skills; and from the third he sought to learn effective leadership principles.

Eventually, he was able to meet and form relationships with these three men, but not until he had been studying them from a distance for years. Each of these ministers played an important mentoring role for him and helped him develop in various areas of his life.

May God help us all to follow good examples and to be good examples.

Questions for Reflection and Discussion

1. Referring to Howard Hendricks' statement (everyone needs a Paul, a Barnabas, and a Timothy)...

Who has been influential in mentoring you?_____

_____

_____

Who has been a Barnabas (an encourager) to you, and to whom have you been a Barnabas?_____

_____

_____

Who is a Timothy that you've poured your life into?_____

_____

_____

Are you working to cultivate these types of relationships in your life?

_____

_____

2. As you reviewed the list of traits of spiritual fathers, how many of those characteristics are present in your life?_____

_____

_____

_____

_____

_____

_____

_____

_____

_____

3. What is the main insight that you have gained from this chapter?

_____

_____

_____

_____

_____

_____

_____

_____

_____

_____

_____

_____

MINISTRY KILLERS YOU MUST CONQUER- THE GRIND

Chapter Twenty-Two

DEALING
WITH BURNOUT

"Working too long without a break is a form of pride."[53]

- Dave Williams

Key Thought: *Spiritual leaders who last learn how to pace themselves, take breaks, and find rejuvenation during the journey.*

Many begin their work in ministry with zeal, eagerness, enthusiasm, and idealism. After all, what could be a greater honor than being called to work for God, and what could be more fulfilling and rewarding than serving God's people? While some maintain vibrancy and high energy over the long-haul, many spiritual leaders inadvertently "hit the wall" at some point in their journey. According to one survey, "45.5 percent of pastors say that they've experienced depression or burnout to the extent that they needed to take a leave of absence from ministry."[54]

They may not have seen it coming, yet they reached a point of depletion and found themselves running on fumes. For too long, they had given, given, and given... far more than they had taken in. They had not replen-

---

[53]Williams, Dave, *Emerging Leaders*, (Lansing, MI: Decapolis Publishing, 2005), 115.
[54]London Jr., H.B., and Wiseman, Neil B., *Pastors at Greater Risk*, (Ventura, CA: Regal Books, 2003), 172.

ished themselves or taken sufficient breaks. Perhaps they had gotten so busy ministering to others that they forgot to monitor their own spiritual and emotional health. Maybe they tried to live up to impossible expectations (imposed by themselves or by others) or got worn down dealing with difficult, uncooperative, or unappreciative people. Disappointments and disillusionment can chip away at the morale of a spiritual leader, and over time, they find themselves just trying to keep their own head above water.

What is burnout? Frank Minirth and Paul D. Meier describe burnout as, "… a loss of enthusiasm, energy, idealism, perspective, and purpose. It can be viewed as a state of mental, physical, and spiritual exhaustion brought on by continued stress."[55] One dictionary says it is "exhaustion of physical or emotional strength or motivation usually as a result of prolonged stress or frustration."[56]

Dr. Richard A. Swenson speaks of burnout in the "Charred Bacon" section of his book, *Margin*. He writes, "Next time you fry bacon, leave one strip in the pan for an extra fifteen minutes. Then pick it up and look it over. This shriveled, charred, stiff-ended strip is analogous to what a person experiences in burnout." Some of the symptoms and attitudes of burnout include:

- Exhaustion

- Depression

- Irritability, hostility

- Paranoia, suspiciousness

- Withdrawal, noninvolvement

- Multiple psychosomatic illnesses

---

[55]Minirth, Frank, and Meier, Paul D., *How to Beat Burnout*. (Chicago, IL: Moody Press, 1986), 15.
[56]www.merriam-webster.com

- Attitude of "I can't stand this work anymore"

- "I dread going to work"

- "I'd rather be alone"

- "I don't care"

- "I hate it"[57]

Gregory of Nazianzus, who ministered in the fourth century, appears to have been dealing with burnout when he said, "I am spent, O my Christ, Breath of my life. Perpetual stress and surge, in league together, make long, oh long this life, this business of living. Grappling with foes within and foes without, my soul hath lost its beauty, blurred your image."

Long before Gregory voiced his experience, prominent biblical figures, on occasion, expressed varying levels of anguish, frustration, hopelessness, and despair. Could burnout have been at least a contributing factor to the pain behind some of these statements?

- **Moses** - *"I can't carry all these people by myself! The load is far too heavy! If this is how you intend to treat me, just go ahead and kill me. Do me a favor and spare me this misery!"* (Numbers 11:14-15, NLT).

- **Job** - *"I would rather be strangled—rather die than suffer like this. I hate my life and don't want to go on living"* (Job 7:15-16, NLT).

- **Elijah** - *"Then he went on alone into the wilderness, traveling all day. He sat down under a solitary broom tree and prayed that he might die. 'I have had enough, LORD,' he said. 'Take my life, for I am no better than my ancestors who have already died'"* (1 Kings 19:4, NLT).

---

[57]Swenson, Richard A., M.D. *Margin.* (Colorado Springs, CO: NavPress, 1992), 70.

- **Jeremiah** - *"Yet I curse the day I was born! May no one celebrate the day of my birth. Why was I ever born? My entire life has been filled with trouble, sorrow, and shame"* (Jeremiah 20:14, 18, NLT).

- **Paul** - *"For we do not want you to be ignorant, brethren, of our trouble which came to us in Asia: that we were burdened beyond measure, above strength, so that we despaired even of life. When we came to Macedonia, our bodies had no rest, but we were troubled on every side. Outside were conflicts, inside were fears"* (2 Corinthians 1:8; 7:5).

In all of these cases, there were other issues and factors involved other than burnout, but some kind of depletion and exhaustion occurred as these men dealt with the various stress factors in their lives.

Who is most vulnerable to burnout? Gary R. Collins writes, "Burnout is common in all helping professionals, including the ministry. It occurs most often in perfectionistic people who are idealistic, deeply committed to their work, reluctant to say no, and inclined to be workaholics."[58]

Keys to Preventing and Recovering from Burnout

- **Know the True Nature of God**

How do you perceive God? Some seem to think that God is like the harsh taskmasters of Egypt who were constantly demanding more, more, and more. The Bible says, "So the Egyptians made the Israelites their slaves. They appointed brutal slave drivers over them, hoping to wear them down with crushing labor. So the Egyptians worked the people of Israel without mercy. They made their lives bitter, forcing them to ...do all the work in the fields. They were ruthless in all their demands." (Exodus 1:11, 13-14, NLT).

[58]Collins. Gary R., *Christian Counseling,* (Dallas, TX: Word Publishing, 1988), 35.

If you feel driven and that no matter what you do, it's never enough, then you may have a distorted view of God. Remember that it's the enemy who seeks to drive us with a sense of panic; God leads us with a sense of peace.

It is not wrong to work hard, but make sure that your hard work is prompted by the love of God, and not from a sense of drivenness. "Drivenness is an insatiable drive to do more and be more. It's a drive that may be masked by charitable and positive motives, but in reality it may originate in deep, perhaps even unconscious, feelings of inadequacy and shame."[59]

Consider these scriptures:

He makes me to lie down in green pastures; He leads me beside the still waters. He restores my soul...

Psalm 23:2-3

He will feed his flock like a shepherd. He will carry the lambs in his arms, holding them close to his heart. He will gently lead the mother sheep with their young.

Isaiah 40:11 (NLT)

Are you tired? Worn out? Burned out on religion? Come to me. Get away with me and you'll recover your life. I'll show you how to take a real rest. Walk with me and work with me—watch how I do it. Learn the unforced rhythms of grace. I won't lay anything heavy or ill-fitting on you. Keep company with me and you'll learn to live freely and lightly.

Matthew 11:28-30 (MSG)

---

[59]Robert Hemfelt, Frank Minirth, and Paul Meier, *We are Driven,* (Nashville, TN: Thomas Nelson Publishers, 1991), 6.

Knowing the true nature of God is one thing; however, partaking of His nature is another thing. Psalm 34:8 says, "Oh, taste and see that the LORD is good..." Fellowshipping with God through prayer and feeding on His Word is essential.

- **Establish a Healthy Pace**

When we understand that God is not a harsh taskmaster, who is cracking His whip and making unreasonable demands, then we will be able to settle into a pace that is sustainable for us and those we lead. If we are driven, we will most likely drive others. If we learn to pace ourselves, then we can be a good example and a positive influence on others.

A classic scriptural example of this principle occurred when Jacob met his brother, Esau, after many years of separation. Their relationship had been so strained that Jacob was not really sure how Esau would receive him - would he be hostile or friendly? When the meeting turned out to be amicable, Esau wanted Jacob to travel with him and essentially said, "You follow me, and I'll set the pace for you and those traveling with you." Look at how this played out, and especially how Jacob responded.

> *"Well," Esau said, "let's be going. I will lead the way." But Jacob replied, "You can see, my lord, that some of the children are very young, and the flocks and herds have their young, too. If they are driven too hard, even for one day, all the animals could die. Please, my lord, go ahead of your servant. We will follow slowly, at a pace that is comfortable for the livestock and the children. I will meet you at Seir."*
>
> Genesis 33:12-14 (NLT)

Insecurity, fear, or a desire not to upset Esau could have caused Jacob to ignore the welfare of those entrusted to him. But Jacob demonstrated wisdom and compassion when he said, "We will follow slowly, at a pace that is comfortable for the livestock and the children." Then he essentially said, "We'll get there when we get there, and we'll see you then, but I am not going to hurt those in my care in an attempt to keep up with you, or measure up to your expectations."

Spiritual leaders today would be wise to implement Jacob's strategy. Make sure that you are considering the well-being of your spouse and children as well as that of your workers as you make your journey. Remember, those who love you are affected by your pace. As my friend Gerald Brooks says, "Spiritual leaders need to not only consider their own pain tolerance in ministry, but the pain tolerance of their spouse as well."

Richard A. Swenson said, "We must have some room to breathe. We need freedom to think and permission to heal. Our relationships are being starved to death by velocity. No one has the time to listen, let alone love. Our children lay wounded on the ground, run over by our high-speed good intentions. Is God proexhaustion? Doesn't He lead people beside the still waters anymore?"[60]

• Find the Rhythm God Ordained for Your Life

We have all heard the old addage, "All work and no play makes Jack a dull boy." There is great truth in that. Richard Exley wrote, "Take a minute and think about it. Are you practicing the rhythm of life - that delicate balance between work and rest, worship and play? Are you fulfilled? Are the most important relationships in your life as they should be? Do you take time for yourself? For God? What about play? Are you fun to live with?"[61]

If you have workaholic tendencies, then that statement might be challenging to hear. I was that way. When one is "working for God," it

[60]Swenson, Richard A., M.D. *Margin.* (Colorado Springs, CO: NavPress, 1992), 30.
[61]Exley, Richard, *The Rhythm of Life,* (Tulsa, OK: Honor Books - A Division of Harrison House, 1987), 15.

is easy to neglect other relationships and activities, and seem so virtuous while doing so. However, God did not simply create us to be a working machine that incessantly produces results.

Paul said that God, "...gives us richly all things to enjoy" (1 Timothy 6:17). If that's the case, we should be enjoying natural things, relationships, life, etc. However, we can't do that, if we are exclusively obsessed with work. We need to laugh – a lot! We can't take ourselves too seriously! Everyone else in the church has a life outside of the church, and we need to also. Hobbies can be really helpful in giving the brain a rest from constantly thinking about ministry. Our brains need time to rest and to "re-create!"

Charles Spurgeon wisely said, "Repose is as needful to the mind as sleep to the body... If we do not rest, we shall break down. Even the earth must lie fallow and have her Sabbaths, and so must we. Hence the wisdom and compassion of our Lord, when he said, 'Let us go into the desert and and rest awhile.'" [62] The passage Spurgeon refers to here is Mark 6:31. It reads, "And He said to them, 'Come aside by yourselves to a deserted place and rest a while.' For there were many coming and going, and they did not even have time to eat." Jesus did not advocate pushing harder and harder all the time; He advocated rest.

While we are not under the Old Testament "Law" of the Sabbath, there is a Sabbath principle that remains - and we would be wise to honor it. Breaks are imperative! Small breaks are important, but so are big breaks. Do not short-change yourself on days-off and vacations!

• Take Heed to Yourself

Paul told Timothy, "Take heed to yourself and to the doctrine. Continue in them, for in doing this you will save both yourself and those who hear you" (1 Timothy 4:16).

---

[62]Spurgeon, C.H., *Lectures to My Students*, (Grand Rapids, MI: Zondervan, 1954), 160.

Spiritual leaders are often proficient at taking care of others, but they sometimes neglect taking care of themselves. Working for God is great, but it's not a substitute for properly stewarding and caring for the health of your body, mind, and emotions. How well are you taking care of yourself?

- How is your diet? Are you eating healthy foods?

- How about exercise?

- Are you getting enough rest? Sleeping well?

- When was the last time you saw your doctor or had a physical?

- How is your personal relationship with God? Do you only interact with God relative to your ministry, or do you experience fellowship with Him - feeding on His Word and drawing from His presence - on a personal level?

- What have you done for fun recently? What do you do for fun on a regular basis?

In his outstanding book on burnout, Wayne Cordeiro says, "We don't forget that we are Christians. We forget that we are human, and that one oversight alone can debilitate the potential of our future."[63]

- **Stay Emotionally Healthy**

  How is your soul?

- Do you know your intrinsic value as a child of God? Are you maintaining a sense of positive self-esteem apart from your "performance" and the opinions of others?

- Are you practicing the art of contentment?

---

[63] Cordeiro, Wayne, *Leading on Empty*, (Minneapolis, MN: Bethany House, 2009), 13.

- Are you experiencing joy in your life?

- Do you have a sense of resilience? Do you still have "bounce" in responding to adversity?

- Are you processing emotions well?

- Are you honest about anger, frustrations, and disappointments?

- Have you dealt with unresolved fears in your life? Offense?

- Do you pour your heart out to God, or do you suppress the negatives and keep up the facade?

- Is Psalm 23:3 ("He restores my soul") a reality to you?

Are there any "misbeliefs" that you have that keep you in knots? Are any of the following a part of your self-talk?

- *"God will only love me if I perform perfectly."*

- *"I must have the approval of others in order to feel good about myself."*

- *"If anything goes wrong, it must be my fault."*

- *"I must do everything perfectly."*

- *"I must always be strong and in control."*

- *"No one must see any weaknesses in my life."*

- **Keep the Home Fires Burning**

God has not called us to sacrifice our families on the altar of ministry. Your relationship with your wife and children need to be a priority. You cannot allow yourself to be so drained, emaciated, and exhausted from your ministry, that you have nothing left over to invest at home. You need to have quality time with your spouse, and you should take seriously any warnings or concerns that your spouse expresses.

If you have children or teens, make sure that you are a huge part of their lives. One of the highlights of my life was being able to coach my son's basketball teams when he was young. We were fortunate to work for a Senior Pastor who encouraged all of the staff to be highly involved in their children's lives.

- **Know Your Limits**

Paul said, "We're sticking to the limits of what God has set for us" (2 Corinthians 10:13, MSG). We would do well to do the same. As much as possible, we should focus on what we do well, and through delegation, let others thrive where they are gifted.

If you tend to have an overinflated sense of your own importance, it would be good to remind yourself of the following frequently:

- I am not the Messiah.

- I am not the Holy Spirit.

- I am not indispensable.

- I am not omniscient, omnipotent, or omnipresent.

- I cannot meet every need.

- It's alright for me to establish boundaries and to say "no" to certain things.

- I have permission to delegate and to share the workload with others.

Jesus knew what to say "Yes" to, and what to say "No" to. We see examples in Scripture where He drew boundaries, said "no," and stayed within the limits of His calling.

- Jesus told Peter "no" when he tried to re-direct Jesus' course away from a path that involved suffering (Matthew 16:23).

- He said "no" to the people who wanted to keep Him in one place and prevent Him from preaching in other locations (Luke 4:43).

- Jesus said "no" to the people who wanted to make Him a "natural" king (John 6:15).

Bill Cosby had some good insight when he said, "I don't know the key to success, but the key to failure is trying to please everybody."

- **Receive Ministry**

You may have heard the phrase, "When your outgo exceeds your income, your upkeep becomes your downfall." Some have said this in the context of finances, but this is also true concerning our own spiritual and emotional resources. It is easy to get so involved in giving to and serving others, that a leader simply does not take time to replenish his own inner-reservoir.

> *Jesus... came to a certain village where a woman named Martha welcomed them into her home. Her sister, Mary, sat at the Lord's feet, listening to what he taught. But Martha was distracted by the big dinner she was preparing. She came to Jesus and said, "Lord, doesn't it seem unfair to you that my sister just sits here while I do all the work? Tell her to come and help me." But the Lord said to her, "My dear Martha, you are worried and upset over all these details! There is only one thing worth being concerned about. Mary has discovered it, and it will not be taken away from her."*

> Luke 10:38-42 (NLT)

No one can fault Martha's work ethic, but she went beyond conscientious effort. According to these verses, she was distracted, worried, and upset. Thank God for workers, but we can't work all the time. Jesus saw enormous value in Mary's heart to receive ministry, and called it the "only one thing worth being concerned about."

- **Get a Friend**

Spiritual leaders need someone they can talk with openly, frankly, and candidly. They need someone who they can be real with, someone they don't need to be "professional" with or impress, someone with whom they can be totally transparent and forget about their "image." Typically, this is with another spiritual leader, perhaps a mentor or a counselor, someone who can be trusted.

Isolation is an invitation to disaster for the minister or the believer, and yet 70 percent of pastors indicate that they do not have someone whom they consider a friend.[64] We cannot forget the admonition of Proverbs 27:17, "As iron sharpens iron, so a man sharpens the countenance of his friend."

Concluding Thought

I can't imagine any spiritual leader facing more stress and pressure than the Apostle Paul faced. Among beatings, imprisonments, and shipwrecks, Paul also said, "I have worked hard and long, enduring many sleepless nights. I have been hungry and thirsty and have often gone without food. I have shivered in the cold, without enough clothing to keep me warm" (2 Corinthians 11:27, NLT). In spite of all that, Paul was determined to finish his course with joy (Acts 20:24, KJV). There are two types of spiritual leaders: those who are finishing their course with joy, and those whose course is finishing them. Determine to be in the first group.

---

[64]H.B. London, Jr. and Neil B. Wiseman, *Pastors at Greater Risk.* (Ventura, CA: Regal Books, 2003), 264.

If you are experiencing some level of burnout, please know that God is for you, not against you. He wants to bring rich restoration into your life. Isaiah prophesied of the Messiah saying, "He will not crush the weakest reed or put out a flickering candle" (Isaiah 42:3, NLT).

Isaiah 40:29-31 further speaks of God's restorative nature: "He gives power to the weak, and to those who have no might He increases strength. Even the youths shall faint and be weary, and the young men shall utterly fall, but those who wait on the LORD shall renew their strength; They shall mount up with wings like eagles, they shall run and not be weary, they shall walk and not faint."

As we walk in God's wisdom, I believe that Paul's admonition will be realized in our lives: "Don't burn out; keep yourselves fueled and aflame" (Romans 12:11, MSG). The Amplified Version of this verse says, "Never lag in zeal and in earnest endeavor; be aglow and burning with the Spirit, serving the Lord."

Questions for Reflection and Discussion

1. How do you feel you have done at pacing yourself and replenishing yourself throughout your time of serving God? Has that been a priority and discipline that you've maintained, or have you tended to neglect your own spiritual and emotional well-being while serving others?_____

_____

_____

_____

_____

_____

_____

_____

_____

2. What has your perception of God been? Have you seen Him as a harsh taskmaster, or as a gentle shepherd? Have you felt driven in your work for Him, or have you been led peacefully?_____

_____

_____

_____

_____

_____

_____

_____

3. How well balanced is the rhythm of your life in the areas of worship, work, rest, and play?_____

_____

_____

_____

_____

_____

_____

4. Go back and review the points under "Stay Emotionally Healthy". Do a self-inventory of the bullet points (How is Your Soul?) as well as those dealing with misbeliefs. Are there any adjustments you need to make?

_____

_____

_____

_____

_____

_____

_____

5. What is the main insight that you have gained from this chapter?

_____

_____

_____

_____

_____

_____

_____

_____

_____

MINISTRY KILLERS YOU MUST CONQUER- THE GRINCHES

Chapter Twenty-Three

DEALING WITH
DIFFICULT PEOPLE

"And pray that we'll be rescued from these scoundrels who are trying to do us in. I'm finding that not all 'believers' are believers"

- 2 Thessalonians 3:2, MSG

Key Thought: *Spiritual leaders who do well will have learned how to deal with difficult people.*

Remember the Grinch? The ill-disposed creature, who was determined to ruin Christmas and steal the joy of the citizens of Whoville? Although he managed to swipe their gifts and decorations, the Grinch discovered that the Whos were tremendously resilient, and celebrated the holiday in spite of his scheme. There are grinches that all of us have to deal with – people who will steal our joy if we let them.

I will never forget when one of our Bible school graduates came back and met with me, after he had been out pastoring for a number of years. He said, "When we were in Bible school, I remember being warned several times about not becoming one of those pastors who beat the flock. But you didn't warn us about the congregations who eat their pastors for lunch."

After noting that most church members are kind, caring, and loving, *Pastors at Greater Risks* states that, "...some congregations have an individual or a small group of people who wound pastors and cause horrendous damage in the life of a congregation. Some pastors who've suffered at their hands call these people clergy killers; psychologists might call them pathological antagonists. Generally, they're part of a vocal or controlling minority that causes such chaos that the abused pastor leaves and the congregation is left to pick up the pieces."[65]

Marshall Shelley describes some who cause problems in churches: "Within the church, they are often sincere, well-meaning saints, but they leave ulcers, strained relationships, and hard feelings in their wake. They don't consider themselves difficult people. They don't stay up nights thinking of ways to be nasty. Often they are pillars of the community - talented, strong personalities, deservingly respected - but for some reason, they undermine the ministry of the church. They are not naturally rebellious or pathological; they are loyal church members, convinced they are serving God, but they wind up doing more harm than good." [66]

Shelley proceeds to list several types of people who bring grief to spiritual leaders:

- **The Bird Dog** - always pointing out what others should do

- **The Wet Blanket** - exudes contagious negativity

- **The Entrepreneur** - aggressively uses church connections to build his business

- **The Fickle Financier** - attempts to control the church through giving or withholding finances

---

[65]H.B. London Jr. and Neil B. Wiseman, *Pastors at Greater Risk,* (Ventura, CA: Regal Books, 2003), 57.
[66]Shelley, Marshall, *Well-Intentioned Dragons.* (Waco, TX: Word Books, 1985), 11.

- **The Busybody** - overly involved in everyone else's business

- **The Sniper** - won't say anything face-to-face, but talks about leaders behind their back

- **The Bookkeeper** - Keeps track of every mistake a leader makes

- **The Merchant of Muck** - Attracts other disgruntled people, listens eagerly, and encourages dissatisfaction

- **The Legalist** - Has rigid opinions about how everything should be done[67]

I remember visiting with a pastor years ago, and during the course of our conversation, he made a passing reference to some of his "EGR" members. I wasn't quite sure what he said, so I just kept listening. A few minutes later, he made the "EGR" reference again. This time, I interrupted him and said, "Did you just refer to some of your EGR church members? What does that mean?"

He smiled and said, "I'm sorry - that's a term I use with my staff. It means 'Extra Grace Required.' There are some people who are a bit difficult, and we always look to God for extra grace when we are working with them."

The list from Shelley is just a small sampling of the types of difficult people we might encounter in our journey through life and ministry. Les Parrott identified others in his book entitled, *High Maintenance Relationships*.

- **The Critic** – constantly complains and gives unwanted advice

- **The Martyr** – forever the victim and wracked with self-pity

- **The Wet Blanket** – pessimistic and automatically negative

---

[67]ibid., 37-41.

- **The Steamroller** – blindly insensitive to others

- **The Gossip** – spreads rumors and leaks secrets

- **The Control Freak** – unable to let go and let be

- **The Backstabber** – irrepressibly two-faced

- **The Cold Shoulder** – disengages and avoids conflict

- **The Green-Eyed Monster** – seethes with envy

- **The Volcano** – builds steam and is ready to erupt

- **The Sponge** – constantly in need but gives nothing back

- **The Competitor** – keeps track of "tit for tat"

- **The Workhorse** – always pushes and is never satisfied

- **The Flirt** – imparts innuendoes, which may border on harassment

- **The Chameleon** – eager to please and avoids conflict [68]

Sometimes it's just a minor annoyance to deal with irritating personalities. At other times, it's downright dangerous. Jesus warned His own disciples about dealing with difficult people when He said, "Behold, I send you out as sheep in the midst of wolves. Therefore be wise as serpents and harmless as doves. But beware of men, for they will deliver you up to councils and scourge you in their synagogues" (Matthew 10:16-17).

The Apostle Paul encountered more than his fair share of difficult people. He spoke of experiencing, "many tears and trials" because of religious

---

[68]Parrott III., Les, *High-Maintenance Relationships,* (Wheaton, IL: Tyndale House Publishers. 1996).

opposition (Acts 20:19, NKJV). He said, "I've had to fend off robbers, struggle with friends, struggle with foes. I've been... betrayed by those I thought were my brothers" (2 Corinthians 11:26, MSG).

Twelve Things You Need to Know When Dealing with Difficult People

1. Stay Focused on the Positive

When a person has been hurt in church relationships, it's easy to become jaded and cynical. A person can forget the 100 people who are positive and supportive and become consumed with the one person who is causing pain and difficulty.

Keep a positive attitude and refuse to let detractors steal your joy. Proverbs 3:4 (NLT) says that we can "find favor with both God and people." Jesus no doubt encountered great opposition, but He also experienced great favor with God and man (see Luke 2:52). A spiritual leader cannot afford to develop a victim mentality or a martyr complex. Wallowing in self-pity is not redemptive in any way, and it does not lead to any positive outcomes.

It is important to have healthy friendships! We all need the strength and encouragement that comes from positive fellowship. I've always enjoyed studying relationships in the Bible, especially those involving Paul. In 2 Timothy, in the last epistle that Paul wrote, we can see an amazing cross-section of the people with whom Paul interacted. Let's break these up into two categories.

Negative Relationships Paul Experienced

- *"Everyone from the province of Asia has deserted me—even Phygelus and Hermogenes"* (2 Timothy 1:15, NLT).

- *"Hymenaeus and Philetus ...have left the path of truth... they have turned some people away from the faith"* (2 Timothy 2:17-18, NLT).

- *"Demas has deserted me because he loves the things of this life..."* (2 Timothy 4:10, NLT).

- *"Alexander the coppersmith did me much harm..."* (2 Timothy 4:14).

- *"The first time I was brought before the judge, no one came with me. Everyone abandoned me"* (2 Timothy 4:16, NLT).

How much abandonment and abuse should one person have to take? Paul could have easily been deeply discouraged by everything that he had experienced, and yet there is a tone of triumph in his last epistle. Certainly Paul had strong faith, but he also remained very aware of the positive relationships in his life, even when some of those involved people at a distance. Paul did not allow himself to be obsessed with the negative; he basked in the richness of his friendships.

Positive Relationships Paul Experienced

- *"Timothy, my dear son"* (2 Timothy 1:2, NLT).

- Onesiphorus - *"...he often visited and encouraged me ...he searched everywhere until he found me ...you know very well how helpful he was in Ephesus"* (2 Timothy 1:16-18, NLT).

- *"Luke is with me..."* (2 Timothy 4:11, NLT).

- *"Mark... will be helpful to me in my ministry"* (2 Timothy 4:11, NLT).

- Paul mentioned Tychicus (2 Timothy 4:12, NLT). In Ephesians 6:21 (NLT), he called him, *"...a beloved brother, faithful minister, and fellow servant in the Lord."*

- Paul referred to Priscilla and Aquila (2 Timothy 4:19). Elsewhere he spoke of them as his, *"...fellow workers in Christ Jesus, who risked their own necks for my life, to whom... I give thanks"* (Romans 16:3-4, NLT).

- Above all, Paul was grateful for God's faithfulness. *"But the Lord stood with me and gave me strength so that I might preach the Good News... And he rescued me from certain death. Yes, and the Lord will deliver me from every evil attack and will bring me safely into his heavenly Kingdom"* (2 Timothy 4:17-18, NLT).

Perhaps the reason Paul had so much stamina, so much perseverance, and so much resilience, is because He drew so much encouragement and strength from all the positive relationships in his life. He remained thankful and appreciative for the positive, even in the midst of great negativity.

2. Conflict Is Universal

Throughout the Bible, conflict, tension, and friction among people was very common.

- Adam blamed Eve.

- Cain killed Abel.

- Lot's servants couldn't get along with Abraham's servants.

- Jacob and Esau had a massive falling out.

- Joseph was hated by his brothers, betrayed, and sold as a slave.

- Job was tormented and harshly criticized by those who were supposed to have been his friends.

- David had to dodge the spears of Saul.

- David himself later dealt treacherously with Uriah, ignored the rape of his daughter, and had to flee the rebellious uprising of his embittered son, Absalom.

- David spoke of those who hated him with cruel hatred, who hated him without cause, and those who hated him wrongfully (Psalm 25:19; 35:19; 38:19).

- Elijah fled Jezebel's threats.

- Herod tried to kill Jesus when He was a small child.

- As an adult, Jesus was betrayed by one of His own disciples.

- Paul had a falling-out with Barnabas and a face-to-face confrontation with Peter.

- Euodia and Syntyche were co-laborers in the Lord, but had to be exhorted to get along with each other and to resolve their differences.

When under fire, it is tempting for a spiritual leader to think, "If I was only a better leader, this wouldn't be happening." Sometimes it's helpful to know that you're not the first leader to be in a firestorm of conflict. It's also good to know that it's not personal (even though it can feel extremely personal), when people are critical, disgruntled, complaining, etc. This is usually more of a reflection of who they are, and not necessarily a reflection of you or your leadership.

It's also possible to begin thinking, "If I just go to another church, I won't have to face these kinds of problems." However, the problem is that wherever you go, other people are still going to be there, and people are people. You can't escape human nature.

When first century believers were encountering persecution for their faith, Peter admonished them, "Remember that your Christian brothers and sisters all over the world are going through the same kind of suffering you are. In his kindness God called you to share in his eternal glory by means of Christ Jesus. So after you have suffered a little while, he will restore, support, and strengthen you, and he will place you on a firm foundation" (1 Peter 5:9-10, NLT).

Remember, conflict is universal. The question is not whether you will face it; the question is how you will manage it. God has helped many others through such times, and He will help you as well.

3. There Are Two Types of Pain that a Spiritual Leader Will Encounter

The first is the pain of attrition. Attrition refers to a reduction in numbers. The second is the pain of aggression. This refers to people who attack a leader outright.

Paul experienced attrition when he said that, "Everyone from the province of Asia has deserted me—even Phygelus and Hermogenes" (2 Timothy 1:15, NLT). It's also what he experienced when he said, "Demas has deserted me..." (2 Timothy 4:10, NLT).

Even Jesus experienced attrition in His ranks (John 6:66-67, NLT). "At this point many of his disciples turned away and deserted him. Then Jesus turned to the Twelve and asked, 'Are you also going to leave?'" God also experienced attrition in His realm. Remember that one-third of the angels followed Lucifer in his rebellion.

Spiritual leaders want to gather and influence others, so it typically hurts a leader when individuals leave, especially when the departure is unpleasant. Seasoned ministers:

- Do not allow departures to crush them or make them calloused.

- Do not harbor unforgiveness, offense, or bitterness about the past.

- Lead with an "open hand," recognizing that people have a free will and that they sometimes choose to go other directions.

- Know that both the people and the ministry belong to God, not to them.

- Know that not all departures are the same. Some leave in a healthy manner, in the will of God, and that should be celebrated. Even when a departure is not positive, a leader needs to keep a good attitude, make the best of it, and keep moving forward.

- Use departures as a time to evaluate methods, ministry, etc. in order to learn from the situation and make any necessary adjustments without becoming self-condemning.

- Focus on the people who remain, not on the ones who have left.

- Keep casting vision and building teams for the future.

Paul also experienced the pain of aggression.

Alexander the coppersmith did me much harm. May the Lord repay him according to his works. You also must beware of him, for he has greatly resisted our words.

2 Timothy 4:14-15

The Weymouth translation renders this, "Alexander the metal-worker showed bitter hostility towards me..."

Notice in this particular case, Alexander seemed to hate Paul's message. This issue wasn't about Paul per se, it was about the Word of God that he preached. Jesus said, "Do you remember what I told you? 'A slave is not greater than the master.' Since they persecuted me, naturally they will persecute you. And if they had listened to me, they would listen to you" (John 15:20, NLT).

4. When Swimming with Sharks, Don't Bleed

Spiritual leaders who have experienced the pain of attrition and aggression genuinely appreciate and can attest to the truth that Stuart Briscoe articulated as the qualifications of a pastor: "the mind of a scholar, the heart of a child, and the hide of a rhinoceros." [69]

Toughness and resilience are necessary if spiritual leaders are to complete their assignment.

And see, now I go bound in the spirit to Jerusalem, not knowing the things that will happen to me there, except that the Holy Spirit testifies in every city, saying that chains and tribulations await me. But none of these things move me; nor do I count my life dear to myself, so that I may finish my race with joy, and the ministry which I received from the Lord Jesus, to testify to the gospel of the grace of God.

Acts 20:22-24 (NKJV)

The way to be unmoved by criticism and opposition is to be focused on a purpose bigger than your ego. Paul realized that the attacks against him were not personal, and that the persecution he encountered was because of the message he preached. Paul could have avoided all persecution by doing one simple thing: stop preaching the Gospel! Strength of character, though, will cause a person to unflinchingly push forward to do what is right.

Martin Luther recognized how important strength was in spiritual leadership. Having faced bitter opposition himself, he said, "A preacher

---

[69]Shelley, Marshall, *Well-Intentioned Dragons*, (Minneapolis, MN: Bethany House Publishers, 1985), 35.

must be both soldier and shepherd. He must nourish, defend, and teach; he must have teeth in his mouth and be able to bite and fight." While it's true that spiritual leaders "...do not war according to the flesh" (2 Corinthians 10:3) and "...do not wrestle against flesh and blood" (Ephesians 6:12), still, they have to be tough when it comes to dealing with "vicious wolves" (Acts 20:29, NLT).

Toughness was advocated:

- When Paul told the Thessalonians to, *"warn those who are unruly"* (1 Thessalonians 5:14).

- When Timothy was encouraged to *"wage the good warfare"* (1 Timothy 1:18).

- When Paul instructed Titus to, *"Speak these things, exhort, and rebuke with all authority. Let no one despise you"* (Titus 2:15).

- When Jude admonished believers to, *"fight with everything you have in you for this faith entrusted to us as a gift to guard and cherish"* (Jude 3, MSG).

5. When Fighting Dragons, Don't Become One.

Solomon said, "Guard your heart above all else, for it determines the course of your life" (Proverbs 4:23, NLT). When dealing with difficult people, it is essential to guard your heart against bitterness, resentment, and offense. Don't allow a misbehaving person to drag you down to their level. Here are some important things to remember:

- Don't let someone else's problem become your problem.

- Don't let someone else's carnality bring out your carnality.

- Don't let someone else's sin get you into sin.

- Don't live your life reacting to someone else's "flesh" problem. Live your life responding to the power of God's love.

Jonathan Edwards said, "Resolved: that all men should live to the glory of God. Resolved second: that whether others do or not, I will."

Emulating Edwards' example will cause each of us to purpose:

- I will walk in love whether anyone else does or not.

- I will exhibit the fruit of the Spirit whether anyone else does or not.

- I will maintain a godly attitude whether anyone else does or not.

- I will maintain my peace no matter how tumultuous any situation becomes.

6. Don't Assume that People Will Always Reciprocate Your Kindness

Our expectations play a big role in how well we respond to situations. If we expect that people are always going to be gracious, appreciative, and kind to us - then we are probably going to experience disillusionment and disappointment. It's great to have a positive outlook on life, but we should also be realistic in our expectations.

Unfortunately, there are people who are unappreciative and do not show proper gratitude. Perhaps it was Paul's recognition of this fact that caused him to say, "I will gladly spend myself and all I have for you, even though it seems that the more I love you, the less you love me" (2 Corinthians 12:15, NLT).

David was deeply hurt by the way people responded to him. He said, "They repay me evil for good. I am sick with despair" (Psalm 35:12, NLT).

Over the years, I have talked with spiritual leaders who, like David, were upset that people had been so unappreciative toward them. Granted, it's great (and appropriate) when people express gratitude toward those who have ministered to them; however, that cannot be our motivation as spiritual leaders. If we serve for the accolades of man, we may be disappointed. If we serve, though, for the glory and honor of God, we will never be disappointed. Our ultimate reward is in heaven.

In what he called, "The Paradoxical Commandments," Kent Keith wrote:

People are unreasonable, illogical, and self-centered.
Love them anyway.
If you do good, people may accuse you of selfish ulterior motives.
Do good anyway.
If you are successful, you will win false friends and true enemies.
Succeed anyway.
The good you do today will be forgotten tomorrow.
Do good anyway.
Honesty and frankness make you vulnerable.
Be honest and frank anyway.
The biggest men and women with the biggest ideas can be shot down by the smallest men and women with the smallest minds.
Think big anyway.
People favor underdogs but follow only top dogs.
Fight for a few underdogs anyway.
What you spend years building may be destroyed overnight.
Build anyway.
People really need help but may attack you if you do help them.
Help people anyway.

Give the world the best you have, and you'll get kicked in the teeth.

Give the world the best you have anyway.[70]

Someone adapted the above piece slightly and added the following thought: "You see, in the final analysis, it is between you and God; It was never between you and them anyway."

7. Not All Conflicts Will Be Resolved the Way that You Would Like Them To Be

It's good to strive for the best in every relationship, but we do not have the ability to make every relationship turn out exactly as we would like it to. Paul made a very interesting statement about a believer's responsibility concerning relationships: *"If it is possible, as much as depends on you, live peaceably with all men"* (Romans 12:18).

Paul is saying that we should do all we can do to promote positive, healthy, and productive relationships, but notice the two qualifiers he used. First, "if it is possible" (implying that it's not always possible), and second, "as much as it depends on you" (implying that the will, decisions, and actions of other people are involved).

Many have found that even though they did all they could, went the extra mile, and exercised their best people skills, a conflict with another person still did not work out the way that they desired. However, some of those same people found out that when they turned the situation over to God, reconciliation ultimately came, even if it was several years later.

There are times when we have to turn a situation over to God and leave a strained or broken relationship in His hands, trusting Him that over time, healing will occur, but moving forward with God's plan for our lives in the meantime. The bottom line is that we have to do the best with what we have to work with, and trust God for the best results.

---

[70]Keith, Kent, *Anyway: The Paradoxical Commandments: Finding Personal Meaning in a Crazy World,* (New York, NY: G.P. Putnam's Sons, 2001), 16-17.

8. The People Closest to You Have the Greatest Potential to Hurt You

When a spiritual leader experiences conflict with a peripheral person in the church, it can be bothersome. However, when a spiritual leader has conflict with a core person in the church, with someone very close to him, or with a family member who is highly visible in the church, it can be devastating.

Jesus was betrayed with a kiss, and David knew the betrayal of his own son, Absalom.

> *It is not an enemy who taunts me—I could bear that. It is not my foes who so arrogantly insult me—I could have hidden from them. Instead, it is you—my equal, my companion and close friend. What good fellowship we once enjoyed as we walked together to the house of God...*
>
> *His words are as smooth as butter, but in his heart is war. His words are as soothing as lotion, but underneath are daggers!*
>
> Psalm 55:12-14, 21 (NLT)

Did you note the deceptiveness of the person who caused the intense pain revealed in verse 21? Smooth words? Over the years, I've observed that there are three types of people that spiritual leaders need to be wary of:

- The super spiritual

- The super sweet

- The super slick

Anytime a person is extreme in some aspect of their character, I encourage you to simply use caution. When a person, for example, is overly sweet, I've always wondered if it's genuine (and it can be), or if they are compensating for something. We all appreciate a truly kind person, but

I've noticed that some who appear "hyper-sweet," are actually attempting to cover up an underlying mean streak in their character.

Likewise, a person who goes out of his way to impress you with his extreme spirituality may be a train wreck waiting to happen. I remember a young minister telling me that when he was the candidate for a pastoral position, a certain lady gave a prophecy that he was supposed to be their new pastor. He was excited about this confirmation, however, I felt that I should give him a word of caution. I explained that if that lady could prophesy him into the church, she could also prophesy him out of the church.

I'm not against people who are sweet or spiritual. Thank God for such expressions, when they are genuine. It's a problem, though, when people use these traits in an attempt to conceal and further their own personal agendas.

When it comes to the super-slick, watch out for people who come across as big-talking "wheeler-dealers." When a person always has some grandiose project underway and he's continually recruiting people for his cause with lavish promises, then problems are probably ahead.

Don't be paranoid, but realize that some people will attempt to get close to you (as a spiritual leader) in order to gain leverage from their apparent tight relationship with you.

9. Not All Conflicts Are Between a Good Person (You) and a Bad Person (The Other Party)

We like to classify the good guy and the bad guy in every conflict (and of course, we assume that we're always the good guy). But not every conflict is as clear-cut as Cain killing Abel and Judas betraying Jesus. We need to be careful so we don't see everything through a filter of self-justification, especially when we are experiencing conflict with another person.

When I directed a ministerial association, I would occasionally receive a phone call from a pastor who was upset about a staff member. The pastor would focus on negative issues concerning the work of that staff member. Often, he would present the situation as if the offending staff member was like evil Absalom who was rebelling against good King David.

Unbeknown to either party, I would then receive a call a day or two later from that staff member, complaining about difficulties he was experiencing with the senior pastor (the one who had just called complaining about the staff member). The staff member focused on the faults of the pastor, thus presenting himself as faithful young David who was having to serve under evil King Saul.

Usually, both parties were good people who were simply experiencing personality conflicts, and usually, these individuals learned to work with each other. Ephesians 4:2-3 (NLT) says, "Always be humble and gentle. Be patient with each other, making allowance for each other's faults because of your love. Make every effort to keep yourselves united in the Spirit, binding yourselves together with peace." Part of that in the Message Version says, "...steadily, pouring yourselves out for each other in acts of love, alert at noticing differences and quick at mending fences."

Do you remember the big falling out that Paul and Barnabas had over what to do with John Mark (Acts 15:36-40)? Those were two great and noble men. I believe that both were sincere in their convictions, but they had diametrically opposing views and positions. Paul was looking at the situation from a task-oriented perspective, while Barnabas was more people-oriented in his approach.

Their differences, at that moment, seemed completely irreconcilable. However, many years after Paul refused to accept Mark as a part of his team he said, "Get Mark and bring him with you, for he is useful to me for ministry" (2 Timothy 4:11). Thank God that bridge was not permanently burned!

When you have a conflict, search your heart fearlessly and see if there are any adjustments that you need to make. Don't just automatically (and pridefully) assume that you are always 100% right, and the other party is 100% wrong. It never hurts for us to make sure that we are not contributing to the problematic nature of the situation.

In addition, don't make every disagreement into a deal-breaker. If you feel like you have to split paths with someone everytime you have a difference of perspective or opinion, then you are going to end up as a very isolated and lonely individual.

Cutting the other party some slack, especially on non-critical issues, is important in all relationships, especially marriage. Dr. James Dobson said, "A good marriage is not one where perfection reigns; it is a relationship where a healthy perspective overlooks a multitude of 'unresolvables.'" [71]

Dr. Dobson went on to address the frustrations of women, whose husbands were not sensitive to their needs: "My advice is that you change that which can be altered, explain that which can be understood, teach that which can be learned, revise that which can be improved, resolve that which can be settled, and negotiate that which is open to compromise. Create the best marriage possible from the raw materials brought by two imperfect human beings with two distinctly unique personalities. But for all the rough edges which can never be smoothed and the faults which can never be eradicated, try to develop the best perspective and determine in your mind to accept reality exactly as it is. The first principles of mental health is to accept that which cannot be changed." [72]

When you have to tolerate the imperfections of others and need to cut them some slack, remember that they are probably doing the same thing for you.

---

[71] Dobson, James, *What Wives Wish Their Husbands Knew About Women,* (Carol Stream, IL: Tyndale House Publishers, 1975), 146.
[72] ibid.

10. Maintain Your Sense of Vision, Focus, and Purpose, and Don't Become Distracted by Personality Conflicts

When Nehemiah was rebuilding the walls of Jerusalem, he was passionately consumed with a great sense of mission and purpose. At first, his enemies (Sanballat, Tobiah, and Geshem) mocked and criticized him, but when significant progress had been made, they invited him to come and meet with them.

However, Nehemiah saw through their plot, refused their deceitful invitation, and responded, "I am engaged in a great work, so I can't come. Why should I stop working to come and meet with you?" (Nehemiah 6:3, NLT). Nehemiah understood the power of focus. Staying on-track with his mission was a top priority to him.

Marshall Shelley wrote:

Perhaps the greatest damage done by true dragons is not their direct opposition. It's more intangible. They destroy enthusiasm, the morale so necessary for church health and growth. People no longer feel good about inviting friends to worship services. The air is tense, the church depressed, and everyone aware of 'us' and 'them.'
The effect on pastors is equally serious. They sap the pastor's energy and, just as damaging, goad them into reacting instead of acting.
"The real problem isn't so much their overt actions," observes a veteran pastor. 'But they divert your attention and keep you off guard even if they never openly oppose you. You find yourself not planning, not thinking of the future, not seeking a vision for the church – you're just trying to survive.'
If pastors become preoccupied with dragons, afraid to challenge them or at least too concerned about 'fighting only battles that need to be fought,' they often lose their spontaneity and creativity. Change is stifled, growth stunted, and the direction of ministry is set by the

course of least resistance, which as everyone knows, is the course that makes rivers crooked.

If the first casualties in dragon warfare are vision and initiative, the next victim is outreach. When a pastor is forced to worry more about putting out brush fires than igniting the church's flame, the dragons have won, and the ministry is lost.[73]

Jesus faced countless distractions, and yet He stayed focused and on-track. Isaiah spoke prophetically of the Lord Jesus Christ when he said, "For the Lord GOD will help Me; Therefore I will not be disgraced; Therefore I have set My face like a flint, And I know that I will not be ashamed" (Isaiah 50:7).

Paul rested so comfortably in the Lord's commission concerning his life that he also refused to allow the opinions and criticisms of others to unhinge him. His resolve is a great example to follow.

It matters very little to me what you think of me, even less where I rank in popular opinion. I don't even rank myself. Comparisons in these matters are pointless. I'm not aware of anything that would disqualify me from being a good guide for you, but that doesn't mean much. The Master makes that judgment.

1 Corinthians 4:3-4 (MSG)

11. Sometimes You Need to Isolate the Problem

Billy Martin was once interviewed and asked what made him a successful manager of a professional baseball team. He replied that on every team there are five players who love you, five who hate you, and fifteen who simply want to play ball. "Being a successful manager," he continued, "is to keep the five who hate you away from the other twenty."[74]

---

[73]Shelley, Marshall, *Well-Intentioned Dragons*, (Waco, TX: Word Books, 1985), 41-42.
[74]Dale, Robert, *Surviving Difficult Church Members*, (Nashville, TN: Abingdon Press, 1984), 35.

Proverbs 22:10 says, "Cast out the scoffer, and contention will leave; Yes, strife and reproach will cease."

Romans 16:17 (NLT) states, "Watch out for people who cause divisions and upset people's faith by teaching things contrary to what you have been taught. Stay away from them."

Titus 3:10 (NLT) says, "If people are causing divisions among you, give a first and second warning. After that, have nothing more to do with them."

I have witnessed several church situations over the years in which there was a chronically disgruntled person in the church. No matter what the church or pastor did, it wasn't right, and there was continual fault-finding, grumbling, and criticism. When the person finally left the church (or was asked to leave), everyone was amazed at how much better the atmosphere in the church became and how much the overall morale of the church improved.

It is regrettable that this type of thing is sometimes necessary, but if people can't be content where they are, it would be in everyone's best interest, if they found another place where they could go and be positive and supportive. Unfortunately, this type of person carries their attitude with them wherever they go; therefore, they usually end up being disgruntled elsewhere.

Spiritual leaders, though, should do all that they can to make relationships work. Asking a person to leave should be a last resort, not a first option.

I was conducting a ministers' meeting many years ago in another country, and we had a question and answer session. Three of the pastors asking questions were from a certain city, and all of their questions had to do with, "Is it okay to kick someone out of the church when they do this," and "Is it okay to kick someone out of the church when they do that?" After a handful of these questions, I reminded them that our purpose in spiritual leadership is not to see how many people we can get out of our churches, but rather how many people we can keep in.

> *And a servant of the Lord must not quarrel but be gentle to all, able to teach, patient, in humility correcting those who are in opposition, if God perhaps will grant them repentance, so that they may know the truth, and that they may come to their senses and escape the snare of the devil..."*
>
> 2 Timothy 2:24-25

12. Pick Your Battles

When Paul wrote Timothy about the qualifications of spiritual leaders (elders), he said, among other things that they must be, "...not violent, ...but gentle, not quarrelsome..." (1 Timothy 3:3). In addition, Paul told Titus that bishops must not be "quick-tempered" (Titus 1:7).

If you have ever encountered people who were contentious, argumentative, had a chip on their shoulder, or were just looking for a fight, then you understand why such people make poor spiritual leaders. They repel and scatter others; they do not attract and gather people. Paul wanted Timothy to avoid this type of interaction and instructed him, "...don't get involved in foolish, ignorant arguments that only start fights" (2 Timothy 2:23, NLT).

There are some minute, insignificant, and peripheral issues that should simply never become a point of controversy. As some have said, there are some hills that are not worth dying on. Pope John XXIII wisely said, "See everything; overlook a great deal; correct a little."

Proverbs 26:17 (NLT) says, "Interfering in someone else's argument is as foolish as yanking a dog's ears." Even Jesus refused to get involved in certain conflicts. When someone asked Jesus to oversee the division of an inheritance, Jesus responded, "Friend, who made me a judge over you to decide such things as that?" (Luke 12:14, NLT). Immediately, Jesus began to address the issue of greed and covetousness, which could have been one of the factors in His refusal to attempt to mediate that dispute.

Folk wisdom even teaches us to avoid unnecessary, unfruitful conflict:

- *Never get into fights with ugly people because they have nothing to lose.*

- *Never wrestle in the mud with a pig. You both get filthy, and the pig loves it.*

- *Never get in a spittin' match with a skunk. Even if you win, you come out smelling bad.*

As spiritual leaders, we would be wise to not react to every little problem. We have a responsibility to deal with matters when the welfare of other believers and the health of the church is at stake. A hireling may flee when the wolf comes, but the shepherd does not (John 10:11-13).

Questions for Reflection and Discussion

1. How is your temperament when it comes to dealing with conflict and with difficult people? Are you more like Velcro (where things stick to you), or more like Teflon (where things slide off of you)?_____

_____

_____

_____

_____

_____

_____

2. Re-read the list of difficult types of people from Marshall Shelley and Les Parrott. Have one, or a few of those types of people, been especially difficult for you to deal with? What skills have you developed in dealing with such people?_____

_____

_____

_____

_____

_____

_____

_____

_____

_____

3. As you read about "Conflict is Universal," and saw that Paul had multiple encounters with difficult people, how did you react to that? What does that say to you about your dealings with difficult people?_____

_____

_____

_____

_____

_____

_____

_____

_____

_____

_____

4. Go back and review point # 5 (When Fighting Dragons, Don't Become One). How are you doing in those areas?_____

_____

_____

_____

_____

_____

_____

_____

_____

_____

5. What is the main insight that you have gained from this chapter?_____

_____

_____

_____

_____

_____

_____

_____

_____

_____

_____

_____

_____

_____

_____

_____

Chapter Twenty-Four

SEASONED
OR POISONED?

"To carry a grudge is like being stung to death by one bee."

- William H. Walton

Key Thought: *Live free from offense; let the challenges of ministry make you better, not bitter.*

H ave you ever noticed how many different stories and references there are in the Bible about God's people encountering situations involving some type of poisoning?

- Exodus 15 – When God's people encountered the bitter waters of Marah, the Lord showed Moses a tree. When it was cast in the waters, they were made sweet (the tree foreshadowed the cross).

- Numbers 21 – Serpents in the wilderness were biting the people. God had Moses put a bronze serpent on a pole; whoever looked on it was healed and lived (see John 3:14-15).

- 2 Kings 4 – Elisha and the sons of the prophets were eating stew when they cried out, "There is death in the pot!" Elisha had them put some flour in the pot, and "there was nothing harmful in the pot."

- Mark 16 – Jesus said that his followers would "take up serpents; and if they drink anything deadly, it will by no means hurt them."

- Acts 28 – After the shipwreck incident, Paul was gathering up sticks for a fire when a viper "fastened on his hand." The natives expected Paul to die, but he shook off the serpent into the fire and suffered no harm.

One of the first things we notice is that God consistently provided His servants with an antidote, protected them from poisoning, and even turned bitterness into sweetness. But I have to ask, why so many stories about bitterness and poisoning? Are there additional lessons, principles, and applications we can draw from these stories?

Not to overly spiritualize these stories, but I am reminded that life is full of experiences that have the potential to embitter us, fill us with resentment, and leave us feeling the ache of regret. I believe that God is just as interested in us being free from that type of poisoning as He was in protecting His people in these biblical accounts.

We have probably all heard the phrase, "life will make us bitter or better," and in the same way, I believe that how we respond to God will determine whether we end up seasoned or poisoned. If anyone ever had a right (naturally speaking) to feel sorry for himself, it was Paul. He had been faithful to God, and yet he was being transported to Rome as a prisoner. He endured the horrible and extended storm at sea that resulted in shipwreck, and even had to swim to shore to survive. It was cold and raining when he was picking up the sticks for the fire, and then a snake bit him. It was not a good month for Paul's ministry newsletter!

In the situation with Paul, I love the fact that he not only shook the snake off his hand into the fire, but shortly after that, he laid his hands on the father of Publius and ministered healing to him, as well as to many others on that island (Acts 28:1-9). So, instead of being poisoned, Paul shook off the snake and ended up taking that same hand—the very one the enemy tried to inject with venom—and used it to bring blessing to others. Paul was truly seasoned by grace, not poisoned by adversity!

What are some of the potential poisonings that we are exposed to today?

- Betrayal – someone you trusted and thought was on your side turns against you

- Disappointment – someone doesn't do what you expected them to do and leaves you frustrated

- Broken promises

- Rejection

- Disrespect

- Ingratitude – you go out of your way to help or serve someone, but your actions are not appreciated and are disregarded

- Someone is insensitive to you or fails to recognize your basic needs

- Criticism

- Someone lies or gossips about you

- Someone undermines you – they work against you instead of with you

- Your convictions and values are disregarded

- People place unreasonable demands and expectations on you, and then belittle you when you can't fulfill them

- False accusations - You are blamed for things that weren't your fault

"All of these are things that can poison us if we let them." How we respond to such potential hurts reminds me of this widely circulated story that you may have heard. (I don't know its original author)

Shake It Off and Step Up

There once was a farmer who owned an old mule. The mule fell into the farmer's well one day. The farmer heard the mule braying, so he rushed over to see what had happened. After carefully assessing the situation, the farmer decided that neither the mule, nor the well, was worth the trouble of saving. Instead, he called his neighbors together, told them what had happened, and enlisted them to help him haul dirt to bury the old mule in the well and put him out of his misery.

At first, the old mule was hysterical! However, as the farmer and his neighbors continued to shovel and the dirt hit the mule's back ... a thought struck him. It suddenly dawned on him, that every time a shovel load of dirt landed on his back, he could shake it off and step up.

So that's exactly what he did, blow after blow. "Shake it off and step up ... shake it off and step up ... shake it off and step up," he repeated to encourage himself.

It wasn't long before the old mule, battered, dirty and exhausted, stepped triumphantly over the wall of the well. What seemed like it would bury him, actually blessed him, all because of the manner in which he handled his adversity.

How do we know if we are *seasoned* or *poisoned?* Consider some of the following contrasts:

A Seasoned Individual	A Poisoned Individual
Trusts	Paranoid
Open-hearted	Closed-off
Releases hurts	Accumulates hurts
Has scars	Carries wounds
Thankful	Resentful
Heals others	Poisons others
Proactive	Reactive
Resilient (rolls with the punches)	Fragile (no bounce)

What Can We Do?

- **Make a decision.** Make the decision that you will let life season you, not poison you! Someone said, "You make your decisions, and your decisions will make you."

- **Walk in the power of forgiveness.** Dale Carnegie said, "When we hate our enemies we give them power over us - power over our sleep, our appetites, our happiness. They would dance with joy if they knew how much they were worrying us. Our hate is not hurting them at all, but it is turning our days and our nights into hellish turmoil."

- **Live free from envy and embrace a life of gratitude.** A.W. Tozer said, "A grateful heart cannot be cynical."

- **Monitor your expectations.** Are they realistic? Many times, the sense of disappointment we experience is intensified by our unrealistic expectations. For example, if we think that every-thing will always go our way and that everyone will always treat us nicely, we're setting ourselves up for disillusionment.

- **See the bigger picture.** Charles Noble said, "You must have long-range goals to keep you from being frustrated by short-range failures." Instead of focusing on immediate situations, we need to consider the long-term perspective, especially the eternal ramifications of our lives. Martin Luther King Jr. said, "We must accept finite disappointment, but we must never lose infinite hope."

I believe that all of these principles are part of finishing our course with joy! May God help each of us as we become well-seasoned followers of Jesus.

Questions for Reflection and Discussion

1. Do you feel that you have been able to stay free from carrying bitterness in your life? What about self-pity? If you have ever had such issues operating in your life, what was the effect on you? How did you overcome and get free from those things?_____

_____

_____

_____

_____

_____

_____

_____

_____

_____

2. Do you feel like you have developed the skills of the "old mule," when you've dealt with negatives?_____

_____

_____

_____

_____

_____

_____

_____

_____

_____

_____

3. Reflecting on A.W. Tozer's quote "A grateful heart cannot be cynical," how is your level of gratitude in life?_____

_____

_____

_____

_____

_____

_____

_____

_____

_____

_____

4. What is the main insight that you have gained from this chapter?

_____

_____

_____

_____

_____

_____

_____

_____

_____

_____

_____

Chapter Twenty-Five

THROWING OUT THE HIGH AND LOW SCORES

"There are as many opinions as there are experts."
- Franklin Delano Roosevelt

Key Thought: *Wise spiritual leaders learn how to reject the poison of criticism, but learn from it, if there is something redemptive in it.*

When I was young, I remember watching certain Olympic events such as figure skating and gymnastics, where judges were involved in scoring the athletes. There was a panel of judges from different countries, and they would always throw out the high and low scores in order to determine the final score. I thought of this in the light of the flattery and criticism (especially the criticism), that we sometimes encounter in life. Wouldn't it be great if we could become well-developed in our ability to throw out unjust criticism as well as ego-inflating flattery?

Have you had someone on your case lately? Do you feel like someone has been appointed as the "Apostle of Correction" over your life? Have you been dealing with unjust and unfair criticism? If you answered "Yes," to any of these questions, then I believe this information will be helpful you. If you will learn how to throw out the low scores, then you will be able to focus on who you really are and what you are really called to do.

Abraham Lincoln certainly had to throw out the low scores, in order to successfully lead the nation during his presidency. In the Lincoln Museum in Springfield, Illinois, there is an area called "The Whispering Gallery," which is a dark and twisted hallway where cruel voices can be heard speaking against the president. These walls are lined with newspaper articles and political cartoons that had slanderously and viciously attacked President and Mrs. Lincoln in very personal ways.

The press referred to Lincoln as a "grotesque baboon," a "third-rate country lawyer" who once split the rails and now splits the Union, a "coarse vulgar joker," a "dictator," an "ape," a "buffoon," and other derogatory names. One of his home-state newspapers even called him, "the craftiest and most dishonest politician that ever disgraced an office in America."[75]

How did Lincoln respond to this seemingly relentless torrent of attacks? He said, "If I were to try to read, much less answer, all the attacks made on me, this shop might as well be closed for any other business. I do the very best I know how - the very best I can; and I mean to keep doing until the end. If the end brings me out wrong, ten angels swearing I had been right would make no difference. If the end brings me out all right, then what is said against me now will not amount to anything."[76]

If Lincoln had taken these criticisms to heart, I don't think he could have ever performed his duties as president. Biblically speaking, Jesus Himself was the object and brunt of so much hatred that He took ownership of an Old Testament passage that says, *"They hated me without a cause"* (John 12:25). Thank God that Jesus stayed focused on carrying out His assignment in spite of the opinions and criticisms of others!

---

[75]Phillips, Donald T., *Lincoln on Leadership*, (New York, NY: Warner Books, 1992), 66.
[76]Burlingame, Michael, *The Inner World of Abraham Lincoln*, (Champaign, IL: University of Illinois Press, 1994), 193-194.

Joseph

Think of the bitterness that was directed toward Joseph during his early life. His brothers sold him into slavery. His boss's wife falsely accused him and got him thrown into prison. A man Joseph had helped in prison (Pharaoh's butler) quickly forgot him in spite of his promise to remember him. If Joseph had taken these things to heart, he would have been a very bitter and demoralized man. Instead, Jacob said of Joseph, "Archers attacked him savagely; they shot at him and harassed him. But his bow remained taut, and his arms were strengthened by the hands of the Mighty One of Jacob, by the Shepherd, the Rock of Israel" (Genesis 49:23-24, NLT).

In order for Joseph to succeed, he had to base his identity and sense of destiny on one thing, and one thing only: God's assignment for his life. He could not base his identity or sense of destiny on the way his brothers treated him, the way Potipher's wife lied about him, his imprisonment, or the forgetfulness of the butler. The only way that we can overcome the fear of rejection is by valuing the constant approval of God over the conditional approval of people. The opinions of others simply cannot be allowed to rule our lives!

David

At some point, young David had to come to terms with the spears that Saul threw at him. One option was to internalize the trauma and say, "There must really be something wrong with me." From this point, he could have spiraled into shame, inferiority, self-doubt, and humiliation. If David had done this, he would have remained a victim of Saul's whims, insecurities, and paranoia. The other option was to tell himself the truth and realize that the spears that were being thrown at him were due to a problem that Saul had within himself. This would have liberated David, to realize that Saul's anger was not a reflection of his worth or value, but rather, was merely an expression of Saul's own unresolved internal dysfunction.

Paul

Another Bible character who was intensely criticized was the Apostle Paul. Even the believers in Corinth were registering their fickle opinions about Paul, relative to other ministers, making Paul an unwilling part of a popularity contest. Imagine the ticker at the bottom of the screen: "If you like Paul better than Apollos or Peter, dial 1-800-YES-PAUL." What was Paul's attitude toward these judgments? He was not moved by their criticism or flattery.

> *As for me, it matters very little how I might be evaluated by you or by any human authority. I don't even trust my own judgment on this point. My conscience is clear, but that doesn't prove I'm right. It is the Lord himself who will examine me and decide.*
>
> 1 Corinthians 4:3-4(NLT)

> *It matters very little to me what you think of me, even less where I rank in popular opinion. I don't even rank myself. Comparisons in these matters are pointless. I'm not aware of anything that would disqualify me from being a good guide for you, but that doesn't mean much. The Master makes that judgment.*
>
> 1 Corinthians 4:3-4 (MSG)

Kenneth E. Hagin said, "Paul had grown in grace to such an extent that he sought only to commend himself to God. He was not influenced or affected by what others thought of him. He did not get in bondage to anybody. It was not a carnal independence — but a saintly dignity. The law of love governed him. He was not easily puffed up, nor was he touchy or resentful. His spirit — where the love of God was shed abroad — dominated him. Immature Christians will feel slighted or puffed up. If they are criticized — or even imagine that they are — they are restless, uneasy, and full of self-pity. On the other hand, if they are noticed and appreciated they feel lifted up and full of self-importance. Baby Christians are self-conscious. And ever conscious of what others are thinking about them. Therefore they are 'tossed to and fro' childishly trying to be popular. The mature believer is God-conscious. And ever conscious about what God's Word says about him and to him. Because he is able to testify with Paul, 'It is a very small thing that I should be judged of you or of man's judgment,' he is free to walk in and voice his convictions."[77]

On a practical level, we should always be open to improvement. This may involve learning from and drawing redemptive benefit, even from criticism. However, at the core level of who we are, we should never allow any criticism to lessen the sense of our intrinsic and infinite worth as God's children. We should never give others the right to demean our value or invalidate our destiny. God is the One who has called us, and He is the One to whom we will ultimately answer.

What can make us vulnerable to the criticisms of others? Often, it's the fear of man. We are called to walk in the reverential fear of God, not to be intimidated and paralyzed by the fear of man. I love Billy Sunday's attitude. He said, "And if you think that anybody is going to frighten me, you don't know me yet."

Fearing people is a dangerous trap, but trusting the LORD means safety.
Proverbs 29:25 (NLT)

---

[77]Hagin, Kenneth E., *Growing Up Spiritually,* (Tulsa, OK: Faith Library Publications, 1976), 41-42.

Fearing man goes beyond fearing physical harm. Many fear rejection, ridicule, or disapproval. Some even become "approval addicts," obsessively pursuing human approval at whatever cost and anxiously brooding over what others think of them. As a matter of fact, the Message version paraphrases Proverbs 29:25, "The fear of human opinion disables; trusting in God protects you from that."

This makes me wonder how much of the Body of Christ - believers and leaders - has been paralyzed and had our potential minimized due to the fear of man. A classic example of the fear of man is found in the way that certain individuals responded to Jesus.

> *Many people did believe in him, however, including some of the Jewish leaders. But they wouldn't admit it for fear that the Pharisees would expel them from the synagogue. For they loved human praise more than the praise of God.*
>
> John 12:42-43 (NLT)

When individuals are ruled by the fear of man, they will shrink from their own convictions and violate their own conscience. We can see from this verse (and perhaps from our own experiences and observations), that peer pressure doesn't simply just affect teenagers. If we are overcome by the fear of human opinion, it is probably because we have magnified man and minimized God in our thinking.

> *I, yes I, am the one who comforts you. So why are you afraid of mere humans, who wither like the grass and disappear? Yet you have forgotten the LORD, your Creator, the one who stretched out the sky like a canopy and laid the foundations of the earth.*
>
> Isaiah 51:12-13 (NLT)

When we reverence God properly in our lives and realize that His opinion is the one that ultimately matters, we will avoid the snare, disability, and paralysis that comes from cringing before the potential disapproval of man.

Jesus exhibited great maturity, even when He was twelve years old. When His parents finally found Him in the Temple, Mary really unloaded on Jesus with much emotion. Luke 2:48 (NLT) records her saying: "Son, why have you done this to us? Your father and I have been frantic, searching for you everywhere."

Not everyone responds well to such a statement, but Jesus' response reveals much:

- He did not respond with arrogance. Arrogance would have said, *"I'll do what I want, when I want, and how I want, and I don't want any lip from you."*

- He did not respond apologetically. An apology would have said, *"I'm so sorry. I'll never do anything ever again that upsets you."*

- He did respond with assertiveness. Jesus simply said (Luke 2:49), *"Did you not know that I must be about My Father's business?"* He was so secure, calm, comfortable, and confident in God's acceptance and approval, that He did not need to bristle with arrogance or cower in intimidation.

If we are insecure in the Father's love and acceptance, then we may try to fill that void in our life with the approval of people. The fallacy of this appears when we recognize that man's love and approval is typically conditional, fickle, and temporal. As a result, we are never truly secure because man's love is subject to change. However, the love of God is unconditional, unchanging, and eternal. In Him, we find true security. That's why it is so much better for us to walk in the reverential fear and awe of God, than to be on the emotional "roller coaster" of seeking man's approval.

> *...God has said, "I will never fail you. I will never abandon you." So we can say with confidence, "The LORD is my helper, so I will have no fear. What can mere people do to me?"*

Hebrews 13:5-6 (NLT)

This is the type of confidence that every child and every servant of God should have.

It is important to realize that freedom from the fear of man does not involve having a haughty attitude that says, "Bless God, I don't care what anybody thinks or says about me." It is one thing to be so secure in the acceptance of God that you do not cringe before human rejection or disapproval. However, it is another thing to have a rebellious, arrogant, and carnally independent attitude that leads one to disregard and disrespect others.

To properly understand what our position should be, we not only need to observe Paul's perspective in 1 Corinthians 4:3 (... it matters very little how I might be evaluated by you), but we also need to hear the balancing wisdom that he expressed later in this same book.

> *So whether you eat or drink, or whatever you do, do it all for the glory of God. Don't give offense to Jews or Gentiles or the church of God. I, too, try to please everyone in everything I do. I don't just do what is best for me; I do what is best for others so that many may be saved.*

1 Corinthians 10:31-33 (NLT)

Did Paul just contradict himself? We know that Paul said elsewhere (Colossians 3:22) not to be a people-pleaser, but now he's describing how he always tries to please everyone. This may be a bit paradoxical, but it is not contradictory. Paul is actually talking about two entirely different issues.

In 1 Corinthians 10, Paul is not describing an insecurity or fear-based pursuit of approval for his own benefit, but rather, a love-based effort to serve others for their benefit.

Notice Paul's qualifiers:

- First, he says we should do things for the glory of God.

- Second, he says we should avoid giving offense or being an unnecessary stumbling block that would keep others from God.

- Third, we see he seeks to please others (not just himself). He does this not for his own personal benefit (to meet a need in his own life) but for the benefit of others that they might be saved.

How have you been doing with the opinions of others? Are there some low scores - even denigrating voices from the past - that you need to throw out? Has there been some "trash talk" thrown your way that you need to rise above? Are there some flattering, high scores that you need to ignore?

Remember that you are simply who God says you are and who God has made you to be. You have nothing to feel inferior about - and nothing to feel puffed up about. You are a person of great value because God says you are. You have great potential because He has gifted and called you. Walk in that, and stay free from the bondage that comes from fearing people.

Questions for Reflection and Discussion

1. Have you learned to recognize and avoid being puffed up by flattery?___

_____

_____

_____

_____

_____

_____

_____

_____

_____

2. Have you ever found yourself disabled by the fear of human opinion? How have you overcome that?_____

_____

_____

_____

_____

_____

_____

_____

_____

_____

_____

3. When dealing with conflict, has it been your tendency to respond apologetically, aggressively, or assertively?_____

_____

_____

_____

_____

_____

_____

_____

_____

_____

_____

4. What is the main insight that you have gained from this chapter? _____

_____

_____

_____

_____

_____

_____

_____

_____

_____

_____

_____

_____

Chapter Twenty-Six

GETTING ALONG

"What! At peace with the Father, and at war with His children?
It cannot be."

- John Flavel

Key Thought: *Pervasive teaching throughout the New Testament reminds us how much value God places on unity and positive relationships in the Body of Christ.*

E very book of the New Testament has something to say about how we are supposed to relate to other people.

- How we are to love and treat each other (encouraging, edifying, etc.)

- How to proactively build positive relationships with each other

- We see individuals navigating through difficult relationships – sometimes well, sometimes not so well

- We are challenged to overcome the inclination to rip each other apart

Let's do a quick scan of the books of the New Testament to see what they tell us about getting along. Sometimes the reference is a commandment. At other times it's an observation or a description, but how we relate to others and the significance of our interpersonal relationships is a major theme of the New Testament.

The Gospel of Matthew

5:9 Blessed are the peacemakers, for they shall be called sons of God.

5: 23-24 Therefore if you bring your gift to the altar, and there remember that your brother has something against you, leave your gift there before the altar, and go your way. First be reconciled to your brother, and then come and offer your gift.

18:15 Moreover if your brother sins against you, go and tell him his fault between you and him alone. If he hears you, you have gained your brother.

The Gospel of Mark

9:50 Salt is good, but if the salt loses its flavor, how will you season it? Have salt in yourselves, and have peace with one another.

The Gospel of Luke

17:1-4 Then He said to the disciples, "It is impossible that no offenses should come, but woe to him through whom they do come! It would be better for him if a millstone were hung around his neck, and he were thrown into the sea, than that he should offend one of these little ones. Take heed to yourselves. If your brother sins against you, rebuke him;

and if he repents, forgive him. And if he sins against you seven times in a day, and seven times in a day returns to you, saying, 'I repent,' you shall forgive him."

The Gospel of John

13:34-35 *A new commandment I give to you, that you love one another; as I have loved you, that you also love one another. By this all will know that you are My disciples, if you have love for one another.*

17:20-23 (NLT) *I am praying not only for these disciples but also for all who will ever believe in me through their message. I pray that they will all be one, just as you and I are one—as you are in me, Father, and I am in you. And may they be in us so that the world will believe you sent me. I have given them the glory you gave me, so they may be one as we are one. I am in them and you are in me. May they experience such perfect unity that the world will know that you sent me and that you love them as much as you love me.*

Acts

2:1 ...*they were all with one accord in one place.*

2:46 *So continuing daily with one accord in the temple, and breaking bread from house to house...*

4:32 *Now the multitude of those who believed were of one heart and one soul.*

20:30 *Also from among yourselves men will rise up, speaking perverse things, to draw away the disciples after themselves.*

Romans

12:18 If it is possible, as much as depends on you, live peaceably with all men.

14:19 Therefore let us pursue the things which make for peace and the things by which one may edify another.

1 Corinthians

3:3-4 ...for you are still carnal. For where there are envy, strife, and divisions among you, are you not carnal and behaving like mere men? For when one says, "I am of Paul," and another, "I am of Apollos," are you not carnal?

6:6 But brother goes to law against brother, and that before unbelievers!

11:18 ...when you come together as a church, I hear that there are divisions among you...

13:4-7 Love suffers long and is kind; love does not envy; love does not parade itself, is not puffed up; does not behave rudely, does not seek its own, is not provoked, thinks no evil; does not rejoice in iniquity, but rejoices in the truth; bears all things, believes all things, hopes all things, endures all things.

2 Corinthians

12:20 For I fear lest, when I come, I shall not find you such as I wish... lest there be contentions, jealousies, outbursts of wrath, selfish ambitions, backbitings, whisperings, conceits, tumults...

13:11 Finally, brethren, farewell. Become complete. Be of good comfort, be of one mind, live in peace;...

Galatians

5:14-15 For all the law is fulfilled in one word, even in this: "You shall love your neighbor as yourself." But if you bite and devour one another, beware lest you be consumed by one another!

5:26 Let us not become conceited, provoking one another, envying one another.

Ephesians

4:1-3 ...walk worthy of the calling with which you were called, with all lowliness and gentleness, with longsuffering, bearing with one another in love, endeavoring to keep the unity of the Spirit in the bond of peace.

4:31-32 Let all bitterness, wrath, anger, clamor, and evil speaking be put away from you, with all malice. And be kind to one another, tender-hearted, forgiving one another, even as God in Christ forgave you.

Philippians

1:27 ...stand fast in one spirit, with one mind striving together for the faith of the gospel...

2:2-4 ...fulfill my joy by being like-minded, having the same love, being of one accord, of one mind. Let nothing be done through selfish ambition or conceit, but in lowliness of mind let each esteem others better than himself. Let each of you look out not only for his own interests, but also for the interests of others.

4:2 I implore Euodia and I implore Syntyche to be of the same mind in the Lord.

Colossians

3:12-13 Therefore, as the elect of God, holy and beloved, put on tender mercies, kindness, humility, meekness, longsuffering; bearing with one another, and forgiving one another, if anyone has a complaint against another; even as Christ forgave you, so you also must do.

1 Thessalonians

5:12-13 And we urge you, brethren, to recognize those who labor among you, and are over you in the Lord and admonish you, and to esteem them very highly in love for their work's sake. Be at peace among yourselves.

2 Thessalonians

1:3 We are bound to thank God always for you, brethren, as it is fitting, because... the love of every one of you all abounds toward each other...

1 Timothy

1:4 ...disputes rather than godly edification.

5:1-3 Do not rebuke an older man, but exhort him as a father, younger men as brothers, older women as mothers, younger women as sisters, with all purity. Honor widows who are really widows.

5:17 Let the elders who rule well be counted worthy of double honor, especially those who labor in the word and doctrine.

6:1 Let as many bondservants as are under the yoke count their own masters worthy of all honor...

2 Timothy

2:24-25 And a servant of the Lord must not quarrel but be gentle to all, able to teach, patient, in humility correcting those who are in opposition...

Titus

3:1-3 Remind them to be subject to rulers and authorities, to obey, to be ready for every good work, to speak evil of no one, to be peaceable, gentle, showing all humility to all men. For we ourselves were also once foolish, disobedient, deceived, serving various lusts and pleasures, living in malice and envy, hateful and hating one another.

Philemon

15-16 For perhaps he departed for a while for this purpose, that you might receive him forever, no longer as a slave but more than a slave — a beloved brother, especially to me but how much more to you, both in the flesh and in the Lord.

Hebrews

10:24-25 (AMP) *And let us consider and give attentive, continuous care to watching over one another, studying how we may stir up (stimulate and incite) to love and helpful deeds and noble activities, Not forsaking or neglecting to assemble together [as believers], as is the habit of some people, but admonishing (warning, urging, and encouraging) one another, and all the more faithfully as you see the day approaching.*

12:14-15 Pursue peace with all people, and holiness, without which no one will see the Lord: looking carefully lest anyone fall short of the grace of God; lest any root of bitterness springing up cause trouble, and by this many become defiled;

James

3:16-18 For where envy and self-seeking exist, confusion and every evil thing are there. But the wisdom that is from above is first pure, then peaceable, gentle, willing to yield, full of mercy and good fruits, without partiality and without hypocrisy. Now the fruit of righteousness is sown in peace by those who make peace.

5:16 Confess your trespasses to one another, and pray for one another, that you may be healed.

1 Peter

3:8-9 Finally, all of you be of one mind, having compassion for one another; love as brothers, be tenderhearted, be courteous; not returning evil for evil or reviling for reviling, but on the contrary blessing, knowing that you were called to this, that you may inherit a blessing.

2 Peter

1:5,7 ...giving all diligence, add to your faith... brotherly kindness...

1 John

2:10-11 He who loves his brother abides in the light, and there is no cause for stumbling in him. But he who hates his brother is in darkness and walks in darkness, and does not know where he is going, because the darkness has blinded his eyes.

3:11-12 For this is the message that you heard from the beginning, that we should love one another, not as Cain who was of the wicked one and murdered his brother.

4:20-21 If someone says, "I love God," and hates his brother, he is a liar; for he who does not love his brother whom he has seen, how can he love God whom he has not seen? And this commandment we have from Him: that he who loves God must love his brother also.

2 John

5 And now I plead with you, lady, not as though I wrote a new commandment to you, but that which we have had from the beginning: that we love one another.

3 John

5-8 Beloved, you do faithfully whatever you do for the brethren and for strangers, who have borne witness of your love before the church. If you send them forward on their journey in a manner worthy of God, you will do well, because they went forth for His name's sake, taking nothing from the Gentiles. We therefore ought to receive such, that we may become fellow workers for the truth.

Jude

16 (NLT) These people are grumblers and complainers, living only to satisfy their desires. They brag loudly about themselves, and they flatter others to get what they want.

19-20 These people are the ones who are creating divisions among you. They follow their natural instincts because they do not have God's Spirit in them. But you, dear friends, must build each other up in your most holy faith...

Revelation

2:4 (NLT) But I have this complaint against you. You don't love me or each other as you did at first!

The Bible recognizes that relationships are a two-way street. Remember that Paul told the Romans, "If it is possible, as much as depends on you, live peaceably with all men" (12:18). Even in relationships that don't work well based on the decisions and actions of others, we can still keep our heart right, stay positive, and walk in love. The bottom line is that we can do the right thing and keep a good attitude, even if the other person does not. Our assignment is to do the best that we can in order to cultivate and maintain the best relationships possible.

Questions for Reflection and Discussion

1. Had you ever noticed before how pervasive teaching about relationships was throughout the New Testament? What does this communicate about how God values the way we interact with each other? _____

_____

_____

_____

_____

_____

_____

_____

_____

_____

_____

_____

_____

_____

2. Which scripture(s) speak the most powerfully to you about how God expects us to treat and work with others? _____

_____

_____

_____

_____

_____

_____

_____

_____

_____

_____

_____

_____

_____

_____

3. What is the main insight that you have gained from this chapter?

_____

_____

_____

_____

_____

_____

_____

_____

_____

_____

_____

_____

_____

_____

_____

_____

Chapter Twenty-Seven

TACT AND
DIPLOMACY-

KEYS TO BUILDING (NOT
BURNING) BRIDGES

"Never cut what you can untie."

- Joseph Joubert

Key Thought: *Learning to bring out the best in people and relationships is one of the most important skills a spiritual leader can possess.*

A Case Study of Insensitivity

There was a time in history when the Kingdom of Israel split, but many do not recall what event prompted that division. The split occurred when King Rehoboam demonstrated insensitivity and harshness toward those under his care and answered them roughly.

Rehoboam's influence as a leader was drastically diminished because he lacked diplomacy and tact in dealing with people (he lost 10 of the 12 tribes). The saddest part was that he had been told by wise advisors exactly how to relate properly to those under his care (2 Chronicles 10:7): "If you are kind to these people, and please them, and speak good words to them, they will be your servants forever."

Instead of answering the people harshly, Rehoboam would have been wise to heed the words of Proverbs 15:1, "A soft answer turns away wrath, but a harsh word stirs up anger."

Relationship break-ups can occur for many reasons, however, we don't want to overlook and miss this important lesson concerning tact and diplomacy.

But I Don't Want to Be a People-Pleaser

Many balk at the thought of "pleasing the people," because they think of the insincerity that is spoken of in Colossians 3:23. They don't want to be like the slick, artificial, two-faced flatterers that they have seen who seek to smooth-talk their way to the top. In spite of this, there remains a positive side of pleasing people. Consider these two passages from Paul's writings:

…Just as I also please all men in all things, not seeking my own profit, but the profit of many, that they may be saved. (1 Corinthians 10:33)

Let each of us please his neighbor for his good, leading to edification. (Romans 15:2)

The motive in pleasing people is the key. Paul wasn't in a popularity contest (Galatians 1:10), wasn't obsessed with being politically correct, and he didn't seek to please people for personal gain. Rather, he sought to build bridges that would further Kingdom purposes. He was very deliberate and intentional in this (see 1 Corinthians 9:19-23).

Content, Timing, and Tact

Effective communication, which is one of our greatest tools in building positive relationships, involves three key components:

- **Content** (what we say)

- **Timing** (when we say it)

- **Tact** (how we say it)

Unfortunately, many people have seemingly focused exclusively on content in their communication, while ignoring the vital components of timing and tact. What we say (content) is important, but we are not just told to speak the truth, but to speak the truth in love (Ephesians 4:15). Love doesn't only consider the content or the accuracy of the message, but it also considers the well-being of the hearer and cares enough to seek the best way to communicate the truth. In this chapter, we are focusing on tact and it's essential to realize that even the greatest content can be significantly undermined if we don't exercise wisdom and sensitivity in how we communicate.

Tact is defined as:

- a keen sense of what to say or do to avoid giving offense

- skill in dealing with difficult or delicate situations

- a keen sense of what is appropriate, tasteful, or aesthetically pleasing

- taste

- discrimination

I heard a rather quirky, imaginative story that illustrates the significance of tactfulness. A king called in one of his seers to inquire of his future. The seer answered, "You will live to see all of your sons dead." Hearing this, the king flew into a rage and ordered the seer to be put to death. The king then asked a second seer the same question. This seer said, "You will be blessed with a long life, and die at a ripe old age. You will even outlive all of your family." The king was delighted and rewarded this seer with gold and silver. Both seers reported the same basic fact, but only one of them had tact in the way he communicated his message.

Great Wisdom

In discussing the reasons that ministers fail, Gordon Lindsay said, "... one of the greatest causes of failure is the lack of thoughtfulness or tact. Many ministers have possessed every qualification for service except this one. And why do they lack it? It is largely because they have not taken time to master it. Tact is thoughtfulness of others; it is sensitivity to the atmosphere of the moment; it is a combination of interest, sincerity, and brotherly love—giving the other fellow a sense of ease in one's presence. In a word, it is Christian love—the practice of the golden rule."[78]

Oswald Sanders, another great spiritual leader, said, "The original meaning of the word 'tact' referred to the sense of touch, and came to mean skill in dealing with persons or sensitive situations. Tact is defined as 'intuitive perception, especially a quick and fine perception of what is fit and proper and right.' It alludes to one's ability to conduct delicate negotiations and personal matters in a way that recognizes mutual rights, and yet leads to a harmonious solution."[79]

---

[78]Lindsay, Gordon, *The Charismatic Ministry*, (Dallas, TX: Christ for the Nations, Reprinted 1979), 14.
[79]Sanders, J. Oswald, *Dynamic Spiritual Leadership*, (Grand Rapids: Discovery House Publishers, 1999), 51.

J.G. Randall stated, "Tact is a number of qualities working together: insight into human nature, sympathy, self-control, a knack of inducing self-control in others, avoidance of human blundering, readiness to give the immediate situation an understanding mind and a second thought. Tact is not only kindness, but kindness skillfully extended."

Baltasar Gracian said, "Cultivate tact, for it is the mark of culture... the lubricant of human relationships, softening contacts and minimizing friction."

Bible Commentator Alexander Maclaren remarked, "Kindness makes a person attractive. If you would win the world, melt it, do not hammer it."

Another wisely said, "Tact is the art of making a point without making an enemy."

If any person ever realized that it was impossible to please everyone, it was President Abraham Lincoln. He led the United States through its most difficult and divided days. Realizing the importance of maintaining good relationships whenever possible and avoiding all unnecessary offenses, Lincoln said: "The sharpness of a refusal or the edge of a rebuke may be blunted by an appropriate story so as to save wounded feelings and yet serve the purpose." In other words, Lincoln knew that he had to make tough decisions that not everyone would agree with, but he went out of his way to communicate those decisions and positions in ways that would cause the least amount of damage and would hopefully facilitate ongoing, positive relationships.

Consider the following scriptures that deal with graciousness in communication.

- *The Lord GOD has given me the tongue of the learned, that I should know how to speak a word in season to him who is weary.*
  (Isaiah 50:4)

- *A word fitly spoken is like apples of gold in settings of silver.* (Proverbs 25:11)

- *Pleasant words are like a honeycomb, sweetness to the soul and health to the bones.* (Proverbs 16:24)

- *So all bore witness to Him (Jesus), and marveled at the gracious words which proceeded out of His mouth.* (Luke 4:22)

- *Let your speech always be with grace, seasoned with salt, that you may know how you ought to answer each one.* (Colossians 4:6)

The Limitations of Tact

It would be misleading to give the impression, though, that tactfulness and diplomacy are magic wands that guarantee unqualified success in every situation. The fact that you do your part, exercising wisdom and graciousness, is no guarantee that others will automatically act the way that you would like them to. People marveled at the gracious words that were uttered by Jesus, but He was still crucified. John was known as "The Apostle of Love," but he still ended up being exiled to the Isle of Patmos.

Regardless of the reactions of others—whether they do the right thing or not—we still have a responsibility to become the best communicators that we can, walking in kindness and wisdom and doing everything within our power, with God's help, to build the best relationships with people that we possibly can.

May God give us wisdom as we purpose that our words will minister grace to all that hear them.

Questions for Reflection and Discussion

1. Have you ever experienced the reality of Proverbs 15:1 "A soft answer turns away wrath, but a harsh word stirs up anger?"_____

_____

_____

_____

_____

_____

_____

_____

_____

2. How would you rate your own skills in tact and diplomacy? If you need improvement, what areas do you specifically need to work on?

_____

_____

_____

_____

_____

_____

_____

_____

3. What is the main insight that you have gained from this chapter?

_____

_____

MINISTRY KILLERS YOU MUST CONQUER-
THE GOOFINESS

Chapter Twenty-Eight

AVOIDING ERROR, EXTREME, AND IMBALANCES

"Error never shows itself in its naked reality, in order not to be discovered. On the contrary, it dresses elegantly, so that the unwary may be led to believe that it is more truthful than truth itself."[80]

- Irenaeus of Lyons

Key Thought: *Wholesome doctrine and healthy practices should be the trademark of godly spiritual leaders.*

When I first put the "ministry killer" material together, I went through 1 & 2 Timothy to verify that Paul had addressed each of these areas to his protégé, and he did. Here are some scriptures that represent each of these areas:

- **The Gold** - *"...the love of money is a root of all kinds of evil, for which some have strayed from the faith in their greediness, and pierced themselves through with many sorrows"* (1 Timothy 6:10).

---

[80]González, Justo L., *The Story of Christianity: The Early Church to the Dawn of the Reformation,* (New York, NY: HarperCollins Publishers, 2010), 69.

- **The Girls** - *"Flee also youthful lusts; but pursue righteousness, faith, love, peace with those who call on the Lord out of a pure heart"* (2 Timothy 2:22).

- **The Glory** - *"...not a novice, lest being puffed up with pride he fall into the same condemnation as the devil"* (1 Timothy 3:6).

- **The Grind** - *"You therefore, my son, be strong in the grace that is in Christ Jesus...You therefore must endure hardship as a good soldier of Jesus Christ"* (2 Timothy 2:1, 3).

- **The Grinches** - *"Alexander the coppersmith did me much harm. May the Lord repay him according to his works. You also must beware of him, for he has greatly resisted our words"* (2 Timothy 4:14).

When Walt Disney needed a name for a cartoon character that would be zany, clumsy, and a bit less-than-intelligent, he chose the name "Goofy." Goofiness is synonymous with being foolish, wacky, silly, ridiculous, or ludicrous. So we will be using this term to describe beliefs and practices which are extreme, erroneous, and imbalanced.

When I began surveying Paul's letters to Timothy, to locate Scriptures about the goofiness, I was shocked to find out that he said more about the need for solid doctrine than he did about all the other "ministry killers" combined. Consider the following:

When I left for Macedonia, I urged you to stay there in Ephesus and stop those whose teaching is contrary to the truth. Don't let them waste their time in endless discussion of myths and spiritual pedigrees. These things only lead to meaningless speculations, which don't help people live a life of faith in God. The purpose of my instruction is that all believers would be filled with love that comes from a pure heart, a clear conscience, and genuine faith. But some people have missed this whole point. They have turned away from these things and spend their time in meaningless discussions. They want to be known as teachers of the law of Moses, but they don't know what they are talking about, even though they speak so confidently.

1 Timothy 1:3-7 (NLT)

...a bishop (superintendent, overseer) must ...be a capable and qualified teacher.

1 Timothy 3:2 (AMP)

Now the Spirit expressly says that in latter times some will depart from the faith, giving heed to deceiving spirits and doctrines of demons, speaking lies in hypocrisy, having their own conscience seared with a hot iron...

1 Timothy 4:1-2

If you instruct the brethren in these things, you will be a good minister of Jesus Christ, nourished in the words of faith and of the good doctrine which you have carefully followed. But reject profane and old wives' fables...

1 Timothy 4:6,7

Until I get there, focus on reading the Scriptures to the church, encouraging the believers, and teaching them.

1 Timothy 4:13 (NLT)

Keep a close watch on how you live and on your teaching. Stay true to what is right for the sake of your own salvation and the salvation of those who hear you.

1 Timothy 4:16 (NLT)

Teach these things, Timothy, and encourage everyone to obey them. Some people may contradict our teaching, but these are the wholesome teachings of the Lord Jesus Christ. These teachings promote a godly life. Anyone who teaches something different is arrogant and lacks understanding. Such a person has an unhealthy desire to quibble over the meaning of words. This stirs up arguments ending in jealousy, division, slander, and evil suspicions.

1 Timothy 6:2-4 (NLT)

Timothy, guard what God has entrusted to you. Avoid godless, foolish discussions with those who oppose you with their so-called knowledge. Some people have wandered from the faith by following such foolishness.
1 Timothy 6:20-21 (NLT)

*Hold on to the pattern of wholesome teaching you learned from me...
... carefully guard the precious truth that has been entrusted to you.*
2 Timothy 1:13-14 (NLT)

Remind everyone about these things, and command them in God's presence to stop fighting over words. Such arguments are useless, and they can ruin those who hear them. Work hard so you can present yourself to God and receive his approval. Be a good worker, one who does not need to be ashamed and who correctly explains the word of truth. Avoid worthless, foolish talk that only leads to more godless behavior. This kind of talk spreads like cancer, as in the case of Hymenaeus and Philetus. They have left the path of truth...

2 Timothy 2:14-18 (NLT)

These teachers oppose the truth just as Jannes and Jambres opposed Moses. They have depraved minds and a counterfeit faith. But they won't get away with this for long. Someday everyone will recognize what fools they are, just as with Jannes and Jambres.

2 Timothy 3:8-9 (NLT)

But you must remain faithful to the things you have been taught. You know they are true, for you know you can trust those who taught you.

2 Timothy 3:14 (NLT)

All Scripture is inspired by God and is useful to teach us what is true and to make us realize what is wrong in our lives. It corrects us when we are wrong and teaches us to do what is right.

2 Timothy 3:16 (NLT)

...so proclaim the Message with intensity; keep on your watch. Challenge, warn, and urge your people. Don't ever quit. Just keep it simple. You're going to find that there will be times when people will have no stomach for solid teaching, but will fill up on spiritual junk food—catchy opinions that tickle their fancy. They'll turn their backs on truth and chase mirages.

2 Timothy 4:2-4 (MSG)

Paul clearly and repeatedly taught Timothy that standing up for the truth of God's Word was one of his most important responsibilities. How much more is this necessary for spiritual leaders today? We live in the age of information, and Christians have access to receive more teaching and influence today than at any other time in history. Religious ideas of every form are being promulgated via books, television, radio, magazines, CDs, downloads, and podcasts. Doctrinal perspectives are even presented to believers through social media outlets, such as Facebook and Twitter.

Believers are being influenced by a myriad of outside voices, and some of these voices are neither wholesome or beneficial. It is very concerning to pastors when their members embrace and begin to enthusiastically promote imbalanced and erroneous views to others within their congregation. As spiritual leaders, we want our primary focus to be on proactively promoting truth, not reactively correcting error. We don't want to always be putting out fires and having knee-jerk reactions to every variant idea that comes down the road, and yet, these issues must be addressed.

Some try to minimize the importance of doctrine (teaching), however, doctrine is important because what people believe eventually affects what they do.

It has been said that the most important part of doctrine is its first two letters: do. Doctrine and practice are ultimately intertwined. When Jesus addressed the early churches in Asia Minor, He said that He hated both the doctrine and the deeds of the Nicolaitans (Revelation 2:6, 15).

Libertine teaching isn't simply wrong because it ignores and violates Scripture about holiness and godliness, but also because it facilitates and encourages sinful behavior in its adherents.

Universalism isn't wrong just because it contradicts major biblical teachings about judgment and the need to be born-again. It is also wrong because its error removes the motivation to evangelize. If our teaching isn't ultimately pointing to the finished work of Christ and promoting obedience to the Word of God, then something is wrong.

Paul desired for all believers what he expressed to the Ephesians, "Then we will no longer be immature like children. We won't be tossed and blown about by every wind of new teaching. We will not be influenced when people try to trick us with lies so clever they sound like the truth" (Ephesians 4:14, NLT).

How seriously did Paul take the threat and potential damage of false doctrine? Consider his admonition to the church leaders of Ephesus:

So guard yourselves and God's people. Feed and shepherd God's flock—his church, purchased with his own blood—over which the Holy Spirit has appointed you as elders. I know that false teachers, like vicious wolves, will come in among you after I leave, not sparing the flock. Even some men from your own group will rise up and distort the truth in order to draw a following. Watch out! Remember the three years I was with you—my constant watch and care over you night and day, and my many tears for you."

Acts 20:28-31 (NLT)

A few years ago, I made a list of some observations relative to winds of doctrine. Here are some points from that list.

- Error is not all error. Sometimes the greatest deception is wrapped in a good bit of truth.

- Error capitalizes on areas that have been ignored or neglected by the church.

- The devil's two objectives are for the church to (a) accept the counterfeit, or (b) reject the genuine out of disgust over excesses and abuses involving the counterfeit.

- Error results in establishing an improper consciousness in the people (e.g., more focused on demons than on Jesus, more focused on works than on grace, etc.).

- Error results in establishing an improper dependency in the people.

- Error occurs when there is a major emphasis on minor issues, or a minor emphasis on major issues.

- With error, there is often a strong appeal made to subjective and private elements to substantiate doctrine and methods (e.g., "the Lord told me…"). This often involves "exclusive" and "superior" revelation, which produces isolation and alienation from others.

- With error, basic principles of Bible interpretation are often ignored and neglected.

- Those promoting error often refuse to have their doctrine or methods judged, or show offense if questions are raised. They don't show the open spirit of Paul (Acts 17:11).

- Those promoting error often feel a need to defame and discredit opponents. Also, those who dare question their doctrine are labeled as "persecutors." They are quick to wear the martyr badge if their teaching is challenged.

What steps can a minister take in order to stay balanced in his or her teaching?

- Study! Theology is not a bad word! What's bad is bad theology. Doctrine is not a bad word! What's bad is bad doctrine.

- We need to be rooted and grounded in the great doctrines of the Bible. If we are not established in the great truths of Scripture, then we are more likely to fall for the newest "fad" doctrine that comes down the road.

- In addition to theology, we need to be established in the principles of hermeneutics - properly interpreting Scripture. Being grounded in hermeneutics will encourage us:

  - To read Scripture in its proper historical, cultural, and theological context (be wary of teachings that are presented without solid and significant New Testament support)

  - To avoid false combinations (putting Scriptures together that weren't meant to go together)

  - To avoid placing excessive emphasis on one aspect of Scripture, while neglecting a complementary or balancing aspect of Scripture. Major on the majors and minor on the minors!

- Be accountable! Have some good minister-friends that you can discuss issues with. Encourage them to challenge you, especially if you are considering teaching something that is sensitive or controversial.

- Don't get into pride and feel that you are above accountability and correction, or that people should receive your teaching, because of who you are. Luke (Acts 17:11) commended those believers in Berea who "...searched the Scriptures daily to find out whether these things were so." I've heard some ministers belittle and degrade people for not immediately accepting something that they were saying, instead of commending them for checking things out.

- We must consider the fruit or the application of our doctrine. In expressing deep concern over the gullibility of the Corinthian church, Paul said (2 Corinthians 11:4), "For if he who comes preaches another Jesus whom we have not preached, or if you receive a different spirit which you have not received, or a different gospel which you have not accepted — you may well put up with it!" Notice that Paul wasn't merely concerned about a false gospel, or a distorted perception of Jesus; he was concerned about a "different" spirit. The Holy Spirit has been sent to guide us into all truth. Religious spirits and wrong attitudes must be avoided as much as false doctrine.

- Learn from history! Church history is full of insights about various individuals and groups that have gotten off-track. Not everyone who got into error or became imbalanced was an evil person; many were good, sincere people who may have even started out well before getting off-course.

In his book, *John Alexander Dowie*, Gordon Lindsay addressed factors preceding Dowie's downfall. Lindsay spoke of Dowie's excessive work habits which left him exhausted and led to impaired judgment. He also said that Dowie refrained from taking the counsel of others. Over time, Dowie developed what Lindsay called a "fixation," and said that "practically all false teaching involves a fixation in the mind of the victim who embraces it." Lindsay said, "The Apostle Paul oft repeated the warning that believers should adhere to 'sound doctrine.' The alternative is to ride some 'hobby horse' or get off on some tangent that violates the spirit of evangelical truth—thus dividing the Body of Christ." He further said, "How sad it is to see a man with abilities which, no doubt, could be greatly used by God, lose interest in the great evangelical truths, the salvation of lost souls, and become obsessed with a 'hobby horse' that immobilizes his talents for God, and reduced his value to God and humanity..."[81]

[81]Lindsay, Gordon, *John Alexander Dowie*, (Dallas, TX: Christ for the Nations, Reprint 1980), 206-207.

The great Pentecostal pioneer, Donald Gee wrote in "The Voice of Healing" in 1953, "So many of us are [firmly established] extremists. If we see any ray of truth we push it to such an extreme that our constant pressing of it becomes offensive, vain, and at last erroneous. If we discover any successful line of ministry we run after it to such an extent that it becomes nauseating and exhausted. We are forever missing genuine usefulness by our constant failure to keep well-balanced. In the end men lose confidence in us, our intemperance grieves the Holy Spirit, and we are cast upon the scrap-heap of rejected and unprofitable servants."

Keep a Good Heart

I have long-appreciated the words of Richard Baxter:

"In essentials, unity.
In non-essentials, liberty.
In all things, charity."

In the quest to maintain doctrinal purity, some have become downright mean-spirited. They became self-appointed heresy-hunters who were quick to judge and condemn everyone who disagreed with them, even if it concerned non-essential areas. They had an attitude that they were right and everyone else was wrong. They did very little to build others up to do constructive work in the Kingdom of God; while thriving on tearing others down.

Dr. Bob Cook wisely said, "God reserves the right to use people who disagree with me."

I remember hearing the story of an uneducated preacher, who in the midst of his message, mentioned how the Apostle Paul and his wife, Silas, were in prison in Philippi, and their poor son Timothy was walking up and down the street crying because his mom and dad were in jail. At the end of his message, he gave an altar call and six people came forward and gave their lives to Jesus.

Even though this minister completely misunderstood who Silas was, and missed the fact that Timothy was only Paul's spiritual son, there was still enough truth in his message about Jesus, that the Holy Spirit was able to reach the hearts of these individuals.

God is a "God of Truth," but sometimes God works in spite of some bad doctrine that's in the mix. If God had to wait until all of our doctrine was 100% perfect before He could use us, then we would never get used. It's a serious mistake to think that because someone gets blessed, that this automatically validates 100% of what they are teaching or gives total validation to the minister who is doing the teaching.

We need to be careful so we don't develop a "fighting" attitude, whereby we fail to see the good in people simply because we disagree with part of what they are saying. A great example of a right heart in helping others can found be in the way in which Priscilla and Aquila responded to Apollos.

> *Meanwhile, a Jew named Apollos, an eloquent speaker who knew the Scriptures well, had arrived in Ephesus from Alexandria in Egypt. He had been taught the way of the Lord, and he taught others about Jesus with an enthusiastic spirit and with accuracy. However, he knew only about John's baptism. When Priscilla and Aquila heard him preaching boldly in the synagogue, they took him aside and explained the way of God even more accurately.*

> Acts 18:24-26 (NLT)

Apollos was accurate, as far as he knew, but his knowledge was incomplete. Instead of labeling him as a false teacher or publicly attacking him,

Priscilla and Aquila spent time with Apollos personally and helped him understand some things that he was not acquainted with yet.

Apparently, there were some issues that Paul believed should not have been the focus of "nit-picky" arguments. While he highly valued truth, he said to one church, "Let all who are spiritually mature agree on these things. If you disagree on some point, I believe God will make it plain to you" (Philippians 3:15, NLT). Paul seemed content to just let God show people some things over time, and did not feel the need to try to correct everyone on every little issue.

However, on major issues, Paul was completely ready to fight for the truth of the gospel, especially if was an area that undermined the significance of Christ's finished work. When Paul saw the faith of the Galatian believers being subverted by legalism, he pulled no punches. He said:

> *I am shocked that you are turning away so soon from God, who called you to himself through the loving mercy of Christ. You are following a different way that pretends to be the Good News but is not the Good News at all. You are being fooled by those who deliberately twist the truth concerning Christ. Let God's curse fall on anyone, including us or even an angel from heaven, who preaches a different kind of Good News than the one we preached to you. I say again what we have said before: If anyone preaches any other Good News than the one you welcomed, let that person be cursed.*
>
> Galatians 1:6-9 (NLT)

A wise surgeon knows when to go after a deadly malignancy, but he also knows when to leave a minor condition alone, one that will resolve itself without some drastic intervention. May we receive wisdom and maturity from God in order to handle doctrinal issues with this same kind of wisdom.

Questions for Reflection and Discussion

1. Paul obviously emphasized to Timothy the importance of truth and accuracy in teaching. Is this still essential today? Why or why not?_____

_____

_____

_____

_____

_____

_____

_____

_____

_____

2. How can we stand up strongly for important truths without being mean-spirited and unnecessarily controversial over non-essential matters?_____

_____

_____

_____

_____

_____

_____

_____

_____

_____

3. Go over the list of observations relative to winds of doctrine and see if any of those stand out to you as being especially relevant. Also, can you think of other points that could be included in this list?_____

_____

_____

_____

_____

_____

_____

_____

_____

4. What is the main insight that you have gained from this chapter?_____

_____

_____

_____

_____

_____

_____

_____

_____

_____

_____

_____

_____

_____

_____

Chapter Twenty-Nine

REDEMPTIVE
DISAGREEMENT

ARE YOU MAKING PEARLS
OR JUST GETTING IRRITATED?

"He who has learned to disagree without being disagreeable has discovered the most valuable secret of a diplomat."

- Robert Estabrook

Key Thought: *Spiritual leaders can be kind even when they disagree. We can even learn things through disagreement.*

There is a great lesson in understanding the formation of pearls. Natural pearls are formed when a grain of sand or another object slips in between the two shells of the oyster. Due to the irritating nature of the sand, the oyster encapsulates it in layers of mother of pearl secretion, and the pearl grows in size as the number of layers increase and the iridescent gem is formed.

So the next time you find yourself in disagreement with someone (or someone in disagreement with you), ask yourself this question: *"Am I just getting irritated, or am I making pearls?"* Wisdom teaches us to benefit from disagreements and to make each incident a redemptive growth experience, no matter how irritating it may seem at first.

Heraclitus, the ancient Greek philosopher, said: "The unlike is joined together, and from differences results the most beautiful harmony, and all things take place by strife." My natural reaction to the word "strife" is to recoil against it as something evil and undesirable. There certainly is a toxic form of strife that destroys and injures; however, there is another understanding of this principle that is far less sinister.

When people with good hearts disagree, but are respectful and teachable, then it can be beneficial to both. This is the kind of advantage that is derived from the principle spoken of in Proverbs 27:17 (NLT): "As iron sharpens iron, so a friend sharpens a friend." I have seen wonderful men clash over a disagreement, but because they kept an open-heart and didn't write each other off, they became the best of friends (or resumed a great friendship), and both of them learned and were broadened as a result of what they learned in working through the disagreement.

George Whitfield had a sharp disagreement with John Wesley on the Calvinistic-Arminian issue, yet when Whitfield was asked (antagonistically) if he thought he would see John Wesley in heaven, Whitfield responded, "I fear not, for he will be so near the eternal throne and we at such a distance, we shall hardly get sight of him."

Cultivating the Art of Redemptive Disagreement

I am amazed at the graciousness, character, and maturity that is displayed by Peter after incurring the public rebuke of an angry Apostle Paul. Paul not only corrected Peter in front of the congregation in Antioch, but he also related the event in his epistle to the Galatians, which resulted in this conflict being replayed over and over for believers in countless generations (Galatians 2:11-14).

While Paul was correct doctrinally, it is admirable how Peter so humbly responded. Initially, he probably felt hurt and chafed at the rebuke, but that's something we can only speculate about. However, we do know that he ultimately allowed this experience to make him better, not bitter. Lesser men, who were embarrassed, would have likely held a grudge and been driven to discredit Paul. Nevertheless, Peter allowed the disagreement to season him and refused to let it poison him.

Instead of operating out of insecurity, Peter later honored, and even defended Paul: "This is what our beloved brother Paul also wrote to you with the wisdom God gave him—speaking of these things in all of his letters. Some of his comments are hard to understand, and those who are ignorant and unstable have twisted his letters to mean something quite different, just as they do with other parts of Scripture" (2 Peter 3:15-16, NLT).

When I was younger, it was extremely important to me "to be right." When I graduated from Bible school, I was nearly omniscient (or at least I thought I was), and was on the alert to quickly defeat any belief or idea that did not agree with mine. As I have aged a bit, it's amazing how much less I know now than I did more than 30 years ago! I still hold firmly to certain core beliefs, and I think that is important. However, I have learned to be more respectful of other people's beliefs, ideas, and viewpoints that may not agree with mine. Instead of seeing them as threats to be defeated, I now see them as learning opportunities. I have found it very liberating to embrace the attitude (in many non-essential matters relating to styles, methods, etc.) that, "You don't have to be wrong, for me to be right."

Many wise individuals have learned to benefit, grow, and learn through conflict—they have cultivated the art of redemptive disagreement. Consider the following:

"We find comfort among those who agree with us – growth among those who don't."

– Sydney Harris

"When we are debating an issue, loyalty means giving me your honest opinion, whether you think I'll like it or not. Disagreement at this stage, stimulates me. But once a decision has been made, the debate ends. From that point on, loyalty means executing the decision as if it were your own."

– Colin Powell

"Get a friend to tell you your faults, or better still, welcome an enemy who will watch you keenly and sting you savagely. What a blessing such an irritating critic will be to a wise man, what an intolerable nuisance to a fool!"

– Charles H. Spurgeon

In *The Grace Awakening*, Charles Swindoll shared the following guidelines for modeling grace through disagreeable times:

- Always leave room for an opposing viewpoint.

- If an argument must occur, don't assassinate.

- If you don't get your way, get over it, get on with life.

- Sometimes the best solution is separation.

On the fourth point, Swindoll cited Paul and Barnabas, and said, "If I can't go on with the way things are in a particular ministry, I need to resign! But in doing so I should not drag people through my unresolved conflicts because I didn't get my way. If separation is the best solution, doing it graciously is essential."[82]

---

[82]Swindoll, Charles, *The Grace Awakening*, (Dallas, TX: Word Publishing, 1990), 190.

Questions for Reflection and Discussion

1. How are you when it comes to disagreeing with someone without being disagreeable?_____

_____

_____

_____

_____

_____

_____

_____

_____

_____

2. What is your impression of how Peter was so gracious toward Paul, even after Paul had rebuked him publicly?_____

_____

_____

_____

_____

_____

_____

_____

_____

_____

_____

_____

3. What is the main insight that you have gained from this chapter?_____

_____

_____

_____

_____

_____

_____

_____

_____

_____

_____

_____

_____

_____

Chapter Thirty

THE PERFECT ANTIDOTE—BEING CHRISTOCENTRIC

"Make Christ the diamond setting of every sermon."

- Charles Spurgeon

Key Thought: *Keeping Jesus central and supreme in our lives and ministry is one of the best safeguards spiritual leaders could ever have.*

C hristocentric. I like that term. It simply means that the Lord Jesus Christ is at the center. If Scripture teaches anything, it teaches that Jesus is supreme, pre-eminent, and central in all things.

Colossians 1:16 and 19 in the Message version refers to Jesus and says that "...everything got started in him and finds its purpose in him," and "... everything of God finds its proper place in him." When you look at these verses in a broader context, you can see how strongly Paul emphasizes the centrality of the Lord Jesus Christ.

Christ is the visible image of the invisible God. He existed before any-thing was created and is supreme over all creation, for through him God created everything in the heavenly realms and on earth. He made the

things we can see and the things we can't see—such as thrones, king-
doms, rulers, and authorities in the unseen world. Everything was cre-
ated through him and for him. He existed before anything else, and he
holds all creation together. Christ is also the head of the church, which is
his body. He is the beginning, supreme over all who rise from the dead.
So he is first in everything. For God in all his fullness was pleased to live
in Christ...

Colossians 1:15-18 (NLT)

Each major section of the Bible presents a different aspect regarding Jesus' character, person, and work.

- The Old Testament is preparation for Jesus.

- The Gospels are the manifestation of Jesus.

- The Book of Acts is the propagation of Jesus' message.

- The Epistles are the explanation of Jesus' work.

- The Revelation is the consummation of Jesus' kingdom.

There seems to be a tendency among some, though, to make just about everything central except the Lord Jesus. People often get excited about a teaching, a movement, a doctrine, or a cause, and then place greater emphasis on that one issue than they do upon Jesus himself. Whatever we teach, it must be grounded and centered in the Person of the Lord Jesus Christ. Further, it must lead to His glory and honor.

"People Just Get Bored with Jesus"

Many of my minister-friends remember Pastor Sam Smith. Sam and his wife, Donna, established Faith Christian Center in Seekonk, Massachusetts, and pastored there for many years, before Sam's retirement and departure to heaven. Sam was an outspoken, no-nonsense kind of guy, who loved seeing people get saved. He would often comment on how unfortunate it was that ministers seemed to chase every new wind of doctrine and become obsessed with fads, jumping from one extreme to another. He would remark, "People just get bored with Jesus." What a sad (but true) commentary.

A Christocentric perspective does not mean that we do not teach other biblical truths; it means that we keep Jesus central and supreme in our teaching. For example:

- It is great to teach faith, but we need to remember that Jesus is the Author and the Finisher of our faith (Hebrews 12:2).

- It is important to teach grace, but we must remember that the grace we proclaim is nothing less than the grace of the Lord Jesus Christ (Acts 15:11 and thirteen similar references).

- It is outstanding to teach eschatology, but it is Christ's coming that we anticipate.

- Worship is wonderful, but we don't worship the act of worship; we worship Jesus.

- Leadership is great, but only if we are leading people into a closer relationship with Jesus and more effective service for Him.

- It is tremendous to teach holiness, but we must remember that Jesus is the basis and source of our holiness.

- We want to proclaim and see the gifts of the Spirit in operation, but they are to glorify Christ.

Church history, for example, has witnessed some groups becoming focused on water baptism (and specific beliefs and practices about baptism), almost to the exclusion of other important New Testament emphases. Instead of keeping baptism in its proper context, an "altar" was built around water baptism, and more emphasis was seemingly placed upon it than upon the Lord Jesus Christ himself. Baptism is important; I am not disputing that. However, baptism, in and of itself (without faith in and focus on Jesus) is merely a ritual. Its significance does not exist apart from the Person of the Lord Jesus and its portrayal of our identification with His death, burial, and resurrection. He is what makes baptism important.

Likewise, we have heard teaching on spiritual warfare and demonology that magnifies demons and demonic powers more than the Lord Jesus Christ. Any legitimate teaching should make us more aware of, conscious of, and impressed with Jesus, not with the enemies that He has dethroned and defeated.

Holding Fast to the Head

Paul gave an indication of how we would recognize false teachers (Colossians 2:19). He said that such individuals are, "...not holding fast to the Head," and that is a direct reference to the Lord Jesus. The NLT renders it, "... and they are not connected to Christ, the head of the body." Before we teach or receive teaching, perhaps we should stop and ask certain questions:

• How does this relate to Jesus, the Head?

• How is it connected, and how does it connect us to Him?

• How does it glorify, honor, and exalt Him?

• Does this teaching accurately reflect and represent His words, His work, and His nature?

Jesus was certainly not shy or backward about declaring His own centrality; however, there was not an ounce of arrogance or pride in Him. Jesus simply knew who He was, and what He had come to do. Consider the following:

"You search the Scriptures because you think they give you eternal life. But the Scriptures point to me!"

John 5:39 (NLT)

"I am the way, the truth, and the life. No one comes to the Father except through Me."

John 14:6

And beginning at Moses and all the Prophets, He expounded to them in all the Scriptures the things concerning Himself.

Luke 24:27

" I am the Alpha and the Omega, the Beginning and the End, the First and the Last."

Revelation 22:13

If anyone else made such statements, we would be aghast at their delusional grandiosity and their off-the-charts narcissism, but Jesus was merely speaking the truth.

Being Christocentric in one's theology does not exclude or diminish the importance of the Father or the Holy Spirit. Not only did the Holy Spirit empower Jesus for ministry (Acts 10:38), but Jesus said, "...when the Helper comes... the Spirit of truth... He will testify of Me" (John 15:26). John 16:14 says that the Holy Spirit will bring glory to Jesus by revealing to us whatever He (the Holy Spirit) receives from Jesus.

The Father also drew attention to Jesus when He said, *"This is My beloved Son, in whom I am well pleased. Hear him!"* (Matthew 17:5). Then in Hebrews 1:6 and 9, we read more of God the Father's testimony of Jesus:

- *But when He again brings the firstborn into the world, He says: "Let all the angels of God worship Him."*

- *To the Son He says: "Your throne, O God, is forever and ever; A scepter of righteousness is the scepter of Your kingdom."*

Paul's description of the way in which God the Father honored Jesus is outstanding:

> *...God elevated him to the place of highest honor and gave him the name above all other names, that at the name of Jesus every knee should bow, in heaven and on earth and under the earth, and every tongue confess that Jesus Christ is Lord, to the glory of God the Father.*

> Philippians 2:9-11 (NLT)

We can rest assured that there is no tension, friction, jealousy, or competition among the members of the Trinity; they work in absolute perfect harmony. Whenever you exalt Jesus, you are also honoring the Father and the Spirit. Scripture reveals just how flawless their sense of teamwork is when we learn that the day is coming, "...when he [Jesus] will turn the Kingdom over to God the Father, having destroyed every ruler and authority and power" (1 Corinthians 15:24, NLT).

It would do us well to seriously consider if what we teach is truly drawing people to Jesus and exalting Him as He deserves, or are we guilty of disseminating doctrinal distractions and diversions? Are we bringing clarity or clutter when it comes to His glory, centrality, and preeminence? Jesus is not someone we use to get something else. In other words, He is not merely a "means to an end." Jesus is our "means" and our "end!" He is "the way!" He is our "destination!"

May you be richly blessed as you hold fast to Christ, the Head, and as you keep the Lord Jesus central in all that you do and say.

Questions for Reflection and Discussion

1. Have you ever gotten "bored with Jesus," and made more of other issues than of Him? Have you kept Him central in your life and your ministry?

_____

_____

_____

_____

_____

_____

_____

_____

2. Is it possible to teach other topics and yet still keep Jesus exalted and supreme in what you teach? How is this done?_____

_____

_____

_____

_____

_____

_____

_____

_____

3. What is the main insight that you have gained from this chapter?

_____

_____

_____

_____

_____

_____

_____

_____

_____

_____

_____

_____

_____

_____

Chapter Thirty-One

THE LAW
OF LOVE

"Love is the sum of all virtue, and love disposes us to do good."
- Jonathan Edwards

Key Thought: *Leaders who operate in the highest realm of qualification are those who keep their love walk—loving God and others—at the forefront of all their decisions and actions.*

In writing these pages, I've been continually pondering, *What all do young spiritual leaders need to know to be most effective, to be most qualified?* There are so many things we could have addressed, even practical matters such as manners, common courtesy, truly being respectful and appreciative toward others, writing thank you notes, and so much more.

I thought of Paul's comment to young Timothy, "These things I write to you, though I hope to come to you shortly; but if I am delayed, I write so that you may know how you ought to conduct yourself in the house of God, which is the church of the living God, the pillar and ground of the truth" (1 Timothy 3:14-15).

Knowing how to conduct ourselves in God's house, and while we are doing God's business is huge! If there is one thing that should be stressed in closing, it is God's ultimate law - the law of love. Paul said, "Love never fails" (1 Corinthians 13:8), and those who desire to have a truly lasting ministry with lasting results should make sure that love - God's love - is the basis and the essence of all that they do.

When Jesus was asked about the most important commandment, He responded, "'You must love the LORD your God with all your heart, all your soul, and all your mind.' This is the first and greatest commandment. A second is equally important: 'Love your neighbor as yourself'" (Matthew 22:37-39, NLT).

Instead of trying to keep dozens of regulations, Paul instructed New Testament believers to focus on God's law of love. He said:

> ...he who loves another has fulfilled the law. For the commandments, "You shall not commit adultery," "You shall not murder," "You shall not steal," "You shall not bear false witness," "You shall not covet," and if there is any other commandment, are all summed up in this saying, namely, "You shall love your neighbor as yourself." Love does no harm to a neighbor; therefore love is the fulfillment of the law.
>
> - Romans 13:8-10

I want us to focus on that part of verse 10 that says, *"Love does no harm to a neighbor."* If we are truly walking in love, we will not bring harm or damage to others; love always seeks to edify the other person. If a person is walking in love, he will not engage in destructive gossip, he will not undermine another person, or lie about him.

James said that the law of love was going to be the basis for how we are judged:

> If you really fulfill the royal law according to the Scripture, "You shall love your neighbor as yourself," you do well...So speak and so do as those who will be judged by the law of liberty.
>
> - James 2:8, 12

As you seek to conduct yourself properly in carrying out God's plan, perhaps the most important question you will ever ask yourself is this: What would love do? You will not go wrong ethically if love - the God-kind of love - governs your decisions and your actions.

Here is an inspired checklist about how love acts:

Love endures long and is patient and kind; love never is envious nor boils over with jealousy, is not boastful or vainglorious, does not display itself haughtily.

It is not conceited (arrogant and inflated with pride); it is not rude (un-mannerly) and does not act unbecomingly. Love (God's love in us) does not insist on its own rights or its own way, for it is not self-seeking; it is not touchy or fretful or resentful; it takes no account of the evil done to it [it pays no attention to a suffered wrong].

It does not rejoice at injustice and unrighteousness, but rejoices when right and truth prevail.

Love bears up under anything and everything that comes, is ever ready to believe the best of every person, its hopes are fadeless under all circumstances, and it endures everything [without weakening].

Love never fails [never fades out or becomes obsolete or comes to an end]...

- 1 Corinthians 13:4-8 (AMP)

It's not enough just to mentally agree with these verses and say, "Yes, that's what love does." God wants us to be so transformed and governed by His love that we are able to say, "Yes, that's how I am. That's how I live my life because I allow the love of God, the Word of God, and the Spirit of God to govern all of my decisions and actions."

Another way to evaluate how we're doing is to look at what has been called "The Golden Rule." I love the way one modern paraphrase renders this statement by Jesus:

"Here is a simple rule of thumb for behavior: Ask yourself what you want people to do for you; then grab the initiative and do it for them!"

- Luke 6:31 (MSG)

Ask yourself the question, "Is that the way I would want to be treated if the situation was reversed? Would I want someone saying about me, or doing to me, what I've been saying or doing?"

Someone could list a thousand do's and don'ts, but there are never going to be enough rules and regulations to cover every situation. But if we can learn how to walk in His love, be governed by His Word and Spirit, and truly walk in wisdom, we'll make the right decisions and we'll do the things that glorify God and help people.

The Roman congregation that Paul addressed was comprised of people from different backgrounds, and their different backgrounds were causing the believers there to have differing convictions about certain non-essential matters. When Paul gets to the fourteenth chapter of Romans, he talks to the believers there about not judging each other, not pushing their own convictions on others, and not carrying themselves in a way that would cause a weaker brother to stumble. This would sometimes mean sacrificing one's own personal preferences in favor of what was best for someone else.

Paul then makes a dramatic statement about those who will seek to please God first, honor their brother second, and put their own personal preferences last. He says, "...and whoever in this way devotedly serves Christ, God takes pleasure in him, and men highly commend him" (Romans 14:18, Weymouth).

I can't think of any higher expression of being qualified than that. Seeking the honor and glory of God first, and seeking the benefit and edification of others second. I pray that everyone of us can so run our respective races so that when it is all said and done, God will have taken pleasure in us and men will have highly commended us.

The Prayer of Salvation

God loves you—no matter who you are, no matter what your past. God loves you so much that He gave His one and only begotten Son for you. The Bible tells us that "...whoever believes in him shall not perish but have eternal life" (John 3:16, NIV). Jesus laid down His life and rose again so that we could spend eternity with Him in heaven and experience His absolute best on Earth. If you would like to make Jesus the Lord of your life, say the following prayer out loud and mean it from your heart.

Dear Heavenly Father,

I come to You in the Name of Jesus.

Your Word says, "...the one who comes to Me I will by no means cast out" (John 6:37), so I know You won't cast me out, but You take me in and I thank You for it.

You said in Your Word, "Whoever shall call upon the name of the Lord shall be saved" (Romans 10:13). I am calling on Your Name, so I know You have saved me now.

You also said "...if you confess with your mouth the Lord Jesus, and believe in your heart that God has raised him from the dead, you will be saved. For with the heart one believes unto righteousness; and with the mouth confession is made unto salvation" (Romans 10:9-10). I believe in my heart Jesus Christ is the Son of God. I believe that He was raised from the dead for my justification, and I confess Him now as my Lord.

Because Your Word says, "...with the heart one believes unto righteousness..." and I do believe with my heart, I have now become the righteousness of God in Christ (2 Corinthians 5:21)...And I am saved!

If you prayed the prayer to receive Jesus Christ as your Lord and Savior, please contact us on the web at www.harrisonhouse.com to receive a free book.

The Harrison House Vision

Proclaiming the truth and the power of the gospel of Jesus Christ with excellence;
Challenging Christians to live victoriously, grow spiritually, and know God intimately.

About the Author

Bible teacher and author Tony Cooke has been serving the Body of Christ in various capacities since 1980. His passion for teaching the Bible has taken him to more than forty-five states and to twenty-six nations.

His website (www.tonycooke.org) reaches pastors, missionaries, and other church leaders in more than 180 nations with encouraging and helpful ministerial resources.

Tony was involved in pastoral ministry for more than twenty years, and served as an instructor and the dean of Rhema Bible Training Center. He also served for thirteen years as the director of an International Ministerial Association.

Since 2002, Tony and his wife Lisa have traveled full-time with an assignment of "strengthening churches and leaders."

In addition to being a 1981 graduate of Rhema Bible Training Center, Tony studied Religion at Butler University and received a Bachelor of Science degree in Church Ministries from North Central University.

Tony and his wife, Lisa, reside in Broken Arrow, Oklahoma, and are the parents of two adult children, Laura and Andrew.

To receive free monthly teaching from Tony Cooke, visit www.tonycooke.org and sign up to receive Tony's e-newsletter.